bookworks

bookworks

BOOKS, MEMORY AND PHOTO ALBUMS, JOURNALS AND DIARIES MADE BY HAND

SUE DOGGETT

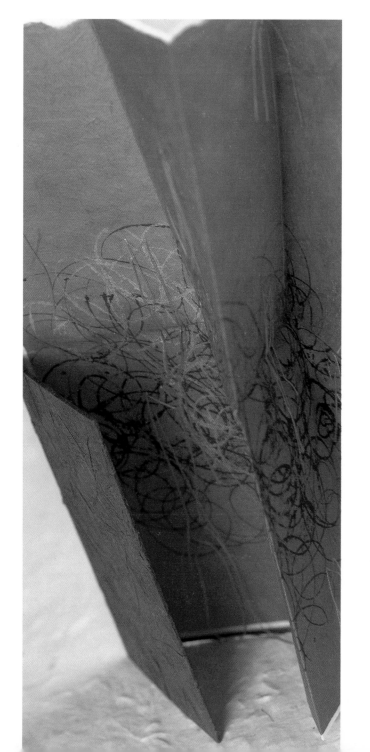

APPLE

A QUINTET BOOK

Published by the Apple Press
6 Blundell Street
London N7 9BH

ISBN 1-84092-090-4

This book was designed and produced by
Quintet Publishing Limited
6 Blundell Street
London N7 9BH

Creative Director: Richard Dewing
Art Director: Clare Reynolds
Designer: Paul Wood
Project Editor: Toria Leitch
Editor: Maggie McCormick
Photographer: Jon Bouchier
Illustrator: Sue Doggett

Typeset in Great Britain by
Central Southern Typesetters, Eastbourne
Manufactured in Singapore by
United Graphic Pte Ltd
Printed in China by
Leefung-Asco Printers Trading Limited

contents

about this book

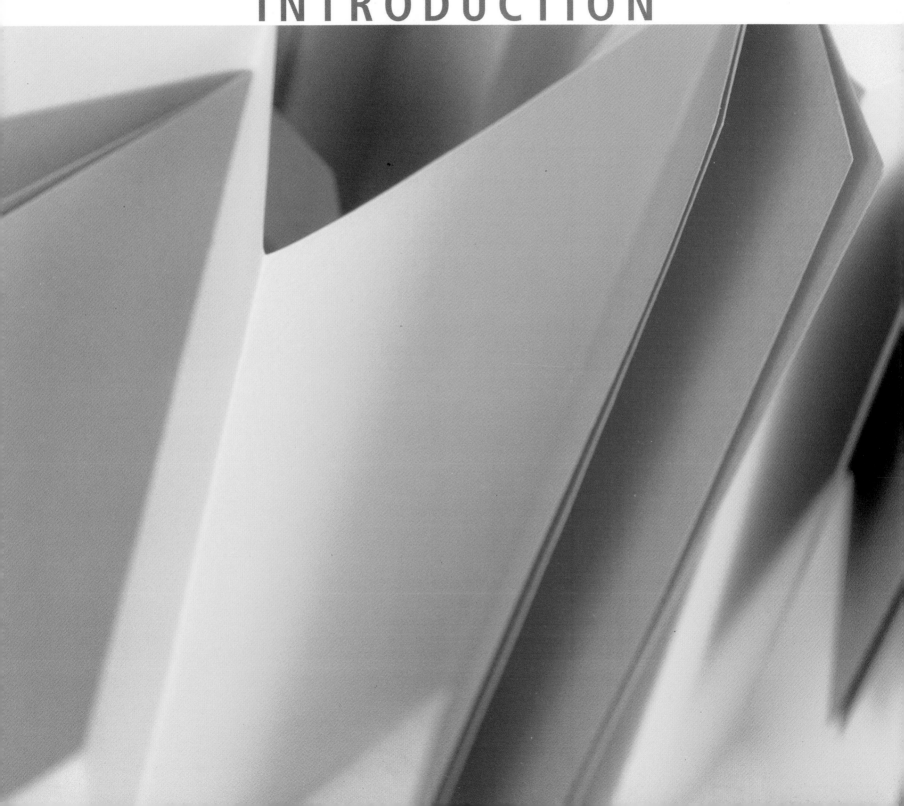

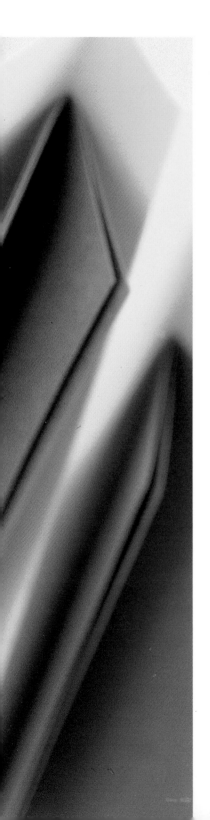

THE BOOK IS A VERY FAMILIAR, TACTILE and interactive object that can be a pleasure to hold, read and write in, especially when it is made well from beautiful and unusual materials.

This book shows you, through step-by-step instructions, diagrams and full-colour illustrations, how you can make your own bookworks using a myriad of wonderful papers, cloths and found materials.

There are chapters dealing with simple folded books, pamphlet stitches, more complex multi-section bindings and containers, all of which can be combined to create your own personalized journals, notebooks, albums and portfolios. There are gallery sections included for inspiration, with examples of work by practising book artists, binders and students, which show ways in which the projects described throughout the book can be developed. The first half of this book deals with getting started, making your own decorative papers, basic techniques and an introduction to different types of book forms, whilst the remaining sections are given over to specific projects. The projects involve many new structures and techniques whilst at the same time utilizing and building upon skills acquired in the earlier chapters. You need only a few basic tools and papers to get started, but of course you can expand your tool box and store cupboard at a later date if you get really hooked! With luck this book will act as a starting point, a springboard for ideas and creative development.

If you need extra information on bookbinding books, and where to buy materials, there is a list of suppliers and useful addresses at the back of the book and a selected bibliography for further reading.

what is a book?

THE HISTORY OF THE BOOK IS RICH and varied, and so closely linked with the development of language, technology and culture that it could be said to be a mirror of society and its history.

The story of the book goes hand in hand with that of writing. From the earliest times, people have always found ways to leave their mark. In the past, all kinds of materials have been used to write on; clay, papyrus, bones, wooden tablets, tree bark, palm leaves and animal skins (notably leather, which is a traditional bookbinding material) have all been used to record information. The earliest examples of clay tablets found were from the Great Temple at Uruk in Sumeria. They date from the fourth millennium BC and are written in cuneiform, a system of writing into wet clay using a wedge-shaped stylus. The Egyptians, famous for their hieroglyphs and papyrus, had been writing since around the thirteenth century BC and the earliest surviving papyrus is about 5,000 years old. The earliest example of Chinese writing is inscribed on bone and belongs to the fourteenth century BC but the most important development attributed to the Chinese concerning the history of the book is the invention of paper in AD 105. Paper remained a closely guarded secret and took many years to reach the West, where parchment (often in the form of highly prized, rare and exclusive illuminated manuscripts) was the most common writing material for books. Paper reached the West via the Silk Route through Turkestan, Syria and Persia; and paper-making factories were set up in Samarkand and Baghdad. Paper-making finally reached Spain in the eleventh century, France in the twelfth century, Fabriano in Italy (still famous today for its hand-made paper) in 1268 and England in the 1490s. The invention of movable type is attributed to Johann Gutenburg in the fifteenth century, although the Chinese already had type in the eleventh century. This invention combined with the use of paper, changed the course of book production for ever. Books became cheaper, more portable and therefore available to more people than ever before. During the following centuries and particularly after the invention of the mechanical press and the paper-making machine in the late eighteenth and early nineteenth centuries, there was a print explosion. Printing on a hand-press could produce 300 sheets a day in the 1780s, while the four-cylinder press invented in 1828 could produce 4,000 sheets an hour.

Books have gone through many changes in form over the centuries to become the structures we now commonly recognize. Coming full circle, we have begun to look again at archaic book forms as a source of inspiration and of re-invention, a counter-argument to using the book purely as a reading machine. To recapture the excitement of handling and reading books is possible by presenting them in an unfamiliar format. They have always been valued for their role in communication and education, and as a record of our varied cultures; but alongside this has been the development of the book as an object of beauty in its own right, encompassing the skills of printers, artists, designers, illustrators, typographers and bookbinders alike. In recent years, the hand-bound book has enjoyed an increasing popularity among artists and makers as a vehicle for visual and artistic expression. There have been new educational courses and workshops established, artists' book fairs, galleries showing more books, books being written about books and there is academic discussion, all of which highlight a continuing intellectual and practical interest in the role of the book in this age of the Internet and computer technology.

The history of the book is not just about grand gestures but personal pleasures too. The excitement you get from writing or drawing for the first time – in a notebook, sketchbook or diary that you have made yourself – is greater than anything you'll get from a glossy shop-bought one. Even the simplest techniques can produce very satisfying results with unusual combinations of colour, texture and materials. Before making anything however, it is a good idea to start with an introduction to how a book works. Familiarity with the terms commonly used in bookbinding, and a knowledge of how books function, will help you to get the most out of this book and the books you make.

book words

THE PROJECTS IN THIS BOOK ARE BASED around two basic structures, one Western and one Eastern: the codex and the concertina fold. The concertina is a simple, beautiful and extensive form that is amazingly versatile. The codex book is a more complex structure in terms of binding and just as exciting to experiment with.

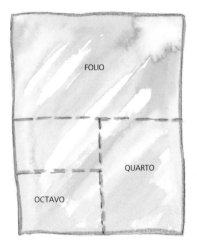

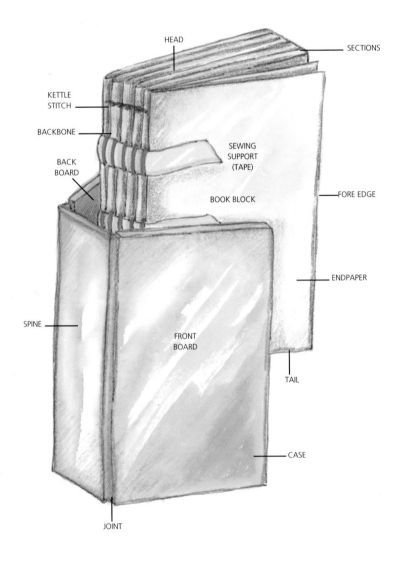

The physical parts of a book are interrelated and they work together to form a structure that has remained essentially unchanged for hundreds of years. The diagram (left) shows the various parts of a codex form with a cover. It is a simplified drawing that shows you the main elements of the structure, giving the common names, which are used throughout this book. You will find additional information on technical terms used in bookbinding in the glossary on the opposite page.

A codex book form consists of a number of sections which are sewn together to form the book block. If a section is printed, or is part of a printed book, it is called a signature. Each section is made from a single sheet of paper, which is folded down and cut to the required size. Each time the paper is folded in half, it is given a different name: folio, quarto and octavo (A). Suitable papers for the projects in this book, and for bookbinding in general, are suggested later in this chapter, under the heading 'Paper'.

glossary

BACK — The edge of the book that is bound.

BEESWAX — Applying beeswax to sewing thread makes it easier to sew with and stronger. Pull the thread through a lump of beeswax a couple of times.

BOARDS — The cover boards of a book.

BOOK BLOCK — The total number of sections making up a book.

CASE — Cover of a case-bound book.

CASING-IN — Process of pasting a book into a case.

CODEX — Book structure sewn in sections along one edge, usually on the fold.

CONCERTINA — Length of paper folded like a fan. Also called accordion, zigzag or leporello fold.

DECKLE EDGE — Ragged, feathery edge of a hand-made sheet of paper.

ENDPAPER — Folded sheets of paper attached to first and last sections of a book for protection. Usually pasted down inside cover boards.

FAN FOLD — Narrow concertina fold.

FORE EDGE — The edges of the pages at the front of the book (opposite the spine).

GRAIN DIRECTION — The direction in which the fibres lie in a piece of machine-made paper.

HEAD — The top edge of a book.

JOINT — The hinge point on a book where the cover board meets the spine.

JOINT ALLOWANCE — The space left between the spine edge of the cover boards and the spine board. Necessary for the cover to open.

KETTLESTITCH — From the German word 'ketteln', meaning to link or make a chain. Sewn at each end of the sections to hold them together.

PASTE DOWN — The outside fold of the endpaper that is pasted to the cover board.

SECTION — A folded and cut sheet of paper. Used either singly or as a unit of a multi-section book.

SEWING SUPPORT — Any tape, cord or other material that supports the sewing of a book. Usually attached or laced in to the cover.

SPINE — The part of a cover that protects the backbone of the book.

SQUARE — Board or covering paper that extends beyond, and protects the pages in, the book.

STIPPLING — Method of gluing in which you hold a large, round-headed brush vertically and move it up and down over the glued area to remove all long, sweeping brush marks.

TAIL — The bottom edge of a book. Also called foot.

TURN-IN — Covering material that turns in over the edges of the cover boards.

WASTE PAPER — Old newspapers or magazines for gluing up on to protect work and work surfaces.

tools and equipment

YOU WILL NEED A FEW BASIC HAND tools to make the most of the projects in this book and many of them are available from art and craft shops. Some tools can also be found in hardware shops, while a few will need to be bought from specialist suppliers. Some of the larger items of equipment listed are optional and, where possible, alternatives have been indicated. However, a bookbinder's press is very useful and using one will give your work a more professional finish. It is sometimes possible to find presses in second-hand shops and flea markets but they are much sought after and it may be easier to contact a bookbinding supplier. Some of these tools can be adapted from household utensils or made from scratch. Alternatives and instructions on how to make them are given where appropriate.

Rulers and Straight Edges

Various steel rulers are available with both metric and imperial measurements. A safety ruler with a recess for your fingers is advisable, especially when cutting boards.

Cutting Tools

Any craft knife will do for cutting paper but a scalpel with a separate handle and blade is preferable. The blades become blunt very quickly and often need changing, so a scalpel is ideal. A sharp blade gives you a better cut and you don't need to press so hard, which means your hand is less likely to slip and the blade less likely to snap. The most useful size blade is 10a.

A Stanley knife has a much thicker, stronger blade and is more suitable for cutting boards.

A cobbler's knife or clip point knife is useful for cutting folds when preparing sections ready for sewing, but a reasonably sharp, blunt-ended kitchen knife would do instead.

A cutting mat keeps your blades from becoming blunt too quickly and protects the work surface. Mats come in various sizes and some have grid marks to help you cut materials square.

Clockwise from top: **Boards, Hole punch, Dividers, Bone Folders, Scalpel, Bodkin, Knife, Brushes, Straight Edge and Chinese scissors.**

Bone Folders

Useful for scoring and folding paper, rubbing down, turning in corners and making boxes. They come in various shapes and sizes, but the single most useful type has a point at one end and is rounded at the other.

Dividers

Dividers enable you to make accurate measurements. Spring dividers that screw open and closed, staying set in the position you require, are the best type to buy.

Set Square

This is for checking before and after cutting that cover boards and other materials are square.

Needles

Bookbinder's size 18 is a good needle to work with, but any long needle with a large eye would be suitable. Curved upholstery needles are useful for winding thread around cords already sewn on to the spine.

Brushes

A large paste brush is essential and it can be used for gluing and pasting, provided you wash it out well after using PVA glue. Smaller brushes for gluing spines and board edges and applying decoration are always useful.

Scissors

You probably already have a large pair of general-purpose scissors around the house, and perhaps a smaller pair such as embroidery scissors or Chinese scissors like the pair pictured are useful for cutting threads and more delicate work.

Pencils and Erasers

It is better to use an HB pencil, or softer, for marking books and paper. The harder grades (H to 6H) leave impressions which are more difficult to erase. Always keep your pencils sharp for a more accurate measurement.

Bodkin or Bradawl

Either is useful for making sewing holes in sections and piercing boards for ties and cords. You can make a bodkin by drilling a hole in the end of a small piece of dowelling and gluing a needle into the hole.

Hammer and Chisel

For making slits for tapes and ties in cover boards etc. You can use a craft knife but do NOT let it slip.

Small Hand Drill

Useful for making holes through thicker boards for sewing on tapes etc.

Hole Punch and Eyelet Maker

For making and finishing holes for ties, ribbons and album posts etc.

Pressing Boards

A few pairs of wooden boards, in various sizes if possible. Make sure the surface of your pressing boards is completely smooth; any lumps or bumps may mark your finished work, especially when it is damp.

Weights

Anything heavy. Books will do but, better still, look out for old flat irons or lead weights. You can also use covered bricks. Remember, the more even the pressure, the better the pressing.

Presses

Bookbinding presses come in various sizes, from small nipping presses to very large standing presses. They are often made of cast iron, but you may also find wooden and aluminium ones.

Paper Cutter

A small paper cutter with a safety bar and a clamp can be useful for trimming book edges, but it is not essential. Most books will look good with roughly cut edges, or with the deckle edge of hand-made paper left untrimmed. You can trim your sections to size with a sharp scalpel before sewing if you wish.

materials

Boards

Many of the projects in this book require boards, for covers and for box-making. You can use almost any card or mount board as long as it is thick enough, especially when you are trying out new projects or practising techniques. However, the best boards to use for finished work are bookbinder's greyboard and millboard. They are both made from good-quality compressed waste and recycled paper. Millboard is denser, tougher and hot-rolled, which means it has a very smooth surface. The less expensive greyboard is excellent for all the projects in this book. Boards come in various thicknesses, ranging from 3 mm (1/16 in) to about 2 mm (3/32 in), the most useful being about 3 mm (1/16 in).

Millboard and greyboard are usually acid-free, but for conservation purposes, archival millboard is guaranteed acid-free and buffered with an agent that stops it from picking up acid from the atmosphere.

Cloth

There is a wide choice of bookbinder's cloth that can be bought by the metre from bookbinding suppliers. Cloth used for covering books and boxes is more hard-wearing than paper, but the choice of colour is much smaller. Some cloths have a waterproof surface which means they can be cleaned; others resemble canvas or fabric. Other fabrics can be used for covering, but if

they are thin or the weave is loose, you will need to apply a backing fabric or paper. This will stop any adhesive from seeping through and spoiling the look of your work. Backing can be applied to the fabric using iron-on interfacing or by gluing a thin piece of paper with PVA glue.

Lining Materials

The materials most commonly used to line the spines of books after sewing are mull, linen and kraft paper. Mull is an open-weave material stiffened with size and is used for strengthening spines, usually in case bindings. Linen is stronger than mull and can be used in the same way. It can also be sewn on to the spine of a pamphlet for a more durable binding. Kraft paper is used for lining spines, boards and boxes, and it is strong and inexpensive. Although the usual colour is brown, it does come in other colours and can be used for artwork and for covering books.

Sewing Materials

You can use all sorts of tapes, thread, cords and ribbons for sewing. Sewing supports depend on your design and what the book is going to be used for. The best thread for strength is bookbinder's linen thread, which is made from flax fibre and comes in various thicknesses. It is usually cream in colour, being unbleached, but you can also buy it in black. If your sewing is going to show and you want a splash of colour, use button thread and apply some beeswax. For case bindings, the best supports to use are linen or cotton sewing tape, which are sold by the roll. Linen tape is unbleached and made from woven flax fibre, while cotton tape is usually bleached. Where the sewing supports are going to show or be part of the design, you can let your imagination run wild. Anything from the haberdashery counter can be used, including leather thongs, ribbons and rubber piping, as long as they are reasonably strong. With all materials, bear in mind what you are going to do with the book and how it is going to be used. The stronger the materials, the longer the book will last.

Found Materials

There are any number of found or easily acquired materials that can be used to enhance your bookworks and boxes. They are often free or cost very little and can be found around the house, in junk and hardware shops and when you're out and about. Curiously twisted driftwood can be used alongside raffia and garden twine as fastenings for journals and albums, and a treasure trove of beads for sewing and finishing can be discovered at local charity shops and second-hand shops. Leaves, wire mesh, carved erasers and combs can be inked and used to print decorative papers, and scraps of treasured hand-made paper can be collaged or sewn together for use as an alternative covering material. Copper and brass wire can be used to decorate clasps, and little pieces of dowelling or wooden skewers make wonderful toggles when carved or painted and polished. Explore the projects in this book and look at the found materials that have been used, particularly in the Scrapbook, the Diary with a Clasp and the gallery pages, which will give you a place to start. Be as inventive as you dare, start collecting and, above all, don't throw anything away. It could end up on a book!

Utility Papers

These are papers used for protection, linings, pressing and wrapping. It is advisable to keep a stock of these papers, many of which can be used more than once, as they will help keep your work clean and give it a better finish.

1. BLOTTING PAPER

This is used for absorbing the dampness from newly pasted endpapers, linings and papers that have been laminated with paste. It can be dried out after use and reused.

2. WAXED PAPER

Keep your work clean and free of glue by using any kind of waxy, silicone-release, greaseproof or plastic-coated paper (such as the backing from self-adhesive covering film) or even sheets of polythene.

3. TISSUE

Acid-free tissue paper is inexpensive and available from paper and bookbinding suppliers. It is a good way of keeping your work clean when it is finished and as interleaving for albums etc.

4. NEWSPRINT

Good for gluing and pasting up delicate work and light-coloured books that will show the dirt.

5. OLD NEWSPAPERS AND MAGAZINES

Keep plenty of these for general gluing and pasting. Less print comes off the colour sections of newspapers and magazines, so they are probably better.

Adhesives

There are two types of adhesive used for the projects in this book, wheatflour paste and PVA glue.

1. PVA GLUE

PVA glue is widely available in craft shops, art shops and bookbinding suppliers. It is used for general bookbinding work, case making, applying covering materials and gluing spines. There are lots of different brands available, but the best bookbinding quality is more flexible than some of the others. It is sold in both an ordinary and a reversible version.

2. PASTE

Paste is used in bookbinding and conservation as it penetrates well due to the high water content. It is also colourless and reversible, which means you can remove it with water. Paste is generally used for laminating two papers together and for putting down endpapers. You can make your own paste at home by following this recipe:

INGREDIENTS

2 rounded dessertspoons of plain wheat flour

½ pint of cold water

METHOD

1. Add a little of the water to the flour and mix to a smooth paste. Add the water little by little to prevent lumps from forming. Keep adding the water until it is all mixed in. If you prefer, the flour and water can be mixed in a blender.

2. Transfer the mixture to a non-metallic saucepan (traces of metal can cause paper to deteriorate over time) and slowly bring to the boil, stirring continuously. The paste will thicken. Reduce the heat and cook for a couple of minutes stirring all the time.

3. Transfer the paste to a container, cover it to stop a skin from forming and leave it to cool. It will keep in the refrigerator for about a week. If you find the paste is too thick, it can be thinned with water, mixing well.

paper

Paper is usually the main component of a book, so it is worth spending some time looking at what it is and how it is made.

The invention of paper is generally attributed to a Chinese emperor's eunuch called Ts'ai Lun, in AD 105. Previously books had been made from silk fibres but he began the process of using beaten fibres, originally hemp and bark, which is the main characteristic of paper.

Paper is made from cellulose, which is derived from broken-down plant fibres such as cotton – with 100 per cent cellulose, it is one of the best materials for papermaking – hemp, wood and flax. Paper was made entirely by hand until the 1800s, when the demand for it increased. Refined wood pulp became a cheaper, more plentiful alternative to cotton and a paper-making machine was invented to speed up the process. The difference between makes and types of paper is vast and their uses are many and various. Paper can be purchased from art shops, craft shops and specialist suppliers, and you can probably buy basic typing paper from your local newsagent. If you can visit one of the larger paper shops or warehouses, you'll be overwhelmed by the splendour and diversity of the papers available from all over the world.

When you are starting out on the first projects, just about any paper will get you going. A good-quality typing paper is a basic material for pages and sections. If you want to use acid-free paper, check the content, since not all papers are. A high acid content usually means the paper is not particularly resistant to light or the atmosphere, and over time will deteriorate more quickly than a paper with a neutral pH value. Acid-free is about 7pH, a balance of acid and alkali. Paper can be divided into three main areas: hand-made, machine-made, and mould-made paper. The method of production for each type of paper is different and the resulting paper has very distinct characteristics.

Hand-made Paper

The process of hand-forming sheets of paper has remained the same for hundreds of years. The fibres are beaten and suspended in water, then removed using a mould and frame called a deckle. The paper-maker moves the mould back

and forth to disperse the fibres and then lets the water drain off. After this, the sheet of paper is transferred to a piece of felt or blanket which is called 'couching'. When enough sheets are piled up between felts, they are pressed to remove the remainder of the water and left to dry. The choice of papers available from the mills of Europe, Japan and India are extraordinary in their variety and beauty. There are special papers for print-making and drawing, and all kinds of colours, textures and designs are available to the book artist. Some papers, such as the Indian Khadi type, include materials as diverse as wool, banana leaf, algae and various grasses, each having an individual appearance. There are Japanese papers with gold flecks and long, silky, swirling fibres, such as Unryu. There are also varieties of paper which are not really paper at all, such as papyrus, made by overlaying crossways strips of the stem of the papyrus plant, and amate which is made from beaten bark (from Mexico and central America), that are ancient in origin. The creative possibilities of all of these papers is endless. Hand-made paper is exciting and rewarding to work with, and although there is a considerable difference in cost between the cheapest and most expensive paper, you can build up a stock of beautiful materials without spending a lot.

Machine-made Paper

The process of producing paper on a machine is very different from that of hand-made paper, and its uses are mainly commercial. The most common source of fibre used in machine paper-making is chemically treated wood pulp. The pulp is placed on a moving bed and is then pressed through a series of rollers and felts. From here the paper is put through a drying machine. It is then sized and dried again before being wound on to a roll, after which it is cut into individual sheets. The size (which is also added to hand-made paper) can be made from gelatine, starch or other chemical compounds. It makes the paper water-resistant and suitable for writing and printing on. There are plenty of machine-made papers useful for making books and many manufacturers make highly coloured, light-resistant and acid-free lines. Mould-made papers are made on a cylinder machine, but the preparation of the high-grade pulp is the same as for hand-made paper.

Grain Direction

There is one characteristic of machine-made paper that is technically very important to the construction of the book. Paper is made on a continuously moving bed, not in individual sheets, so the fibres tend to flow in one direction. This is called the grain direction. If the paper becomes damp – through pasting or gluing, for example – the fibres stretch in the cross direction, at right angles to the grain direction. As the paper dries, it shrinks back and creates a 'pull' on anything the paper is stuck to. It is necessary to control the effects of this pull when binding books so that they are strong and function well. All the materials in a book should have the grain direction running from head to tail, especially on the boards and endpapers where control of the stretch is most vital. Paper folds better with the grain, the pages will open more easily. There are various ways to test for the grain direction:

1. Fold the paper in half lengthways, without creasing it, and apply gentle pressure. Then, fold the paper widthways and feel the difference in the resistance. One way will be springier than the other. The fold with the least resistance is the direction of the grain.

2. Tear a small strip from the corner of a sheet of paper and wet it. The paper will curl because the fibres are expanding. The grain runs in the opposite direction to the curl of the paper.

3. Hold the corner of a piece of paper and pull one edge through the nails of your thumb and index finger in order to stretch it. Do the same with the other edge. The grain direction runs parallel to the edge which stretches the least.

decorating paper

When decorating paper, there are a few aspects that will determine how your finished piece will look. For example, textured and smooth papers will have contrasting finishes, and an absorbent paper will behave totally differently from a coated one. To test the absorbency of a paper, wet the corner and see how long it takes for the water to disappear. The quicker it goes, the more absorbent the paper. Choose papers with qualities that you find appealing, such as their texture, colour, fragility or strength and experiment with the following techniques to make your own personalized covering materials.

All the techniques described below can be used alone or with one another to create a host of unusual effects.

MATERIALS

A selection of papers

Watercolours, poster paint, acrylics and drawing inks

Water-based block-printing ink for monoprinting

Found objects and materials for printing

Paste for papers

Masking fluid

TOOLS

Print rollers for applying colour

Brushes and toothbrushes for painting and spattering

Jars for mixing and storing paint

Wooden skewers and paintbrush ends for drawing into paste papers (explained below)

Card scraps with comb-cut edges for decorating paste papers

Thick sheet of polythene or a piece of glass for inking up

An eye dropper for sprinkling colour (optional)

TECHNIQUES

Sprinkling

1. DRY METHOD

Using an eye dropper or a paintbrush, drip pools of watercolour or ink on to a dry paper, then roll the paper in various directions to run the colour.

2. WET METHOD

Run cold water over your sheet of paper and then drip colour on to the wet areas. It will spread and bleed, giving a spidery effect.

Spattering

Alternatively, using the same techniques as above, use a toothbrush and a knife to sprinkle paint on to the paper for a more delicate effect.

Crumpling and Wash-off

If you crumple the paper carefully after colouring, the ink will settle in the creases, giving an

'antique' feel. Be careful not to use too many different colours at once or you could end up with everything sludge-coloured.

If you let the paint dry a little and then rinse the paper under the tap, you can obtain other interesting effects. The wash-off method can be used with most of the techniques described here. You will find that some paints stain the paper – which is yet another effect to experiment with.

Masking Out

Paint or spatter masking fluid on to your paper (use smooth paper as the fluid will come off more easily) and let it dry. Paint watercolour washes (watered-down colour) over the top and, when they are dry, rub off the masking fluid with an eraser. You will be left with the original paper showing through, which you can either leave or cover with another wash.

Paste Papers

Paste papers are a traditional way of decorating book covers and are fun to make. You will need jars for various colours of poster paint, pieces of card with teeth cut along one edge and blunt tools to draw with. Make a quantity of paste as described in the 'Adhesives' section. Mix one quarter paint to three quarters paste. Use a less absorbent paper for this technique.

Using broad brush strokes, paint the paste mixture on to the paper thinly and evenly. Using any of the drawing tools or card combs, draw will show through where you have drawn. If you don't like what you've done, simply brush over the paste and start again.

Dyeing

The paper for this method should be thin and absorbent, like a strong tissue or Japanese paper. Fold the paper into a zigzag, and then fold this zigzag into another so you end up with a square. Have a few paint colors mixed in jars and dip each corner or edge of the folded paper into the jars alternately. Open up the folded paper, lay it flat, and leave it to dry.

Printing

You can use any of the following methods to print paper you have already colored using other techniques.

1. MONOPRINTING

Use an ink roller to cover a smooth surface like a piece of plastic or glass with block printing ink. Then draw into it with the end of a paint brush. Lay a piece of paper on top of the paint and rub over it with the back of a spoon or your hand. When you peel the paper off, you will have a reverse image of your drawing, called a monoprint because you can only take one print. Making a second printing will sometimes work, but it will be much fainter.

2. PRINTING WITH A ROLLER AND FOUND OBJECTS

Tie string around your roller and then ink up on a piece of glass or plastic. When the roller is inked all around, roll it over your paper and the string print will be transferred. Alternatively, ink up bottle rims, screen wire, leaves, etc., and print by

pressing them down onto your paper.

3. RUBBER STAMPS

Using large plastic erasers to make stamps can produce exciting repeated designs and patterns that look good as borders or for covers and endpapers. Draw your image, a simple shape or letter, on the eraser and cut out the negative areas with a craft knife. Cut away at an angle from the edge of your design so the base is wider than the area you are going to print which will stop the eraser collapsing. Using a stamp pad (available in various colors), print the design on your paper.

Collage

1. PASTING PAPERS

Scraps of paper can be pasted on a full sheet to produce an image or an abstract design. If you are going to use the collage to cover a book or for folding, thinner papers are better because this technique gives two thicknesses of paper laminated together. You can use craft glue or paste to attach the scraps. Paste is probably better, even though it takes longer to dry, because it leaves no residue and can be cleaned off easily. Try photocopying images and designs, and then enlarging or reducing parts of them. Play around with your own drawings and prints by tearing and repositioning them.

2. SEWING PAPERS

Papers can be sewn together either by hand or with machine embroidery. Thinner papers are better if you want to fold the paper at all, but otherwise it is up to you. There are plenty of exciting sewing threads to experiment with,

especially metallic or brightly dyed ones, and some embroidery threads are dyed with different colors on the same skein. You can make it as simple or exotic as you like by varying color schemes. Try using different papers of the same color with contrasting stitching, or multicolored strips or circles or abstract forms. The permutations are endless.

Do's and Don'ts

There are no rules really, but a few hints will help you make sure you get the most out of your tools and materials, and that your work stays looking good when you've finished it.

THINGS TO REMEMBER:

1. If you use acrylic paint to make a print or design, make sure you always have the work wrapped in waxed paper, especially when it is stuck to the book. Acrylic will stick to itself or anything else when it is damp or under pressure.

2. If you are making a paper for a particular project, keep in mind where the paper is going to be used. If it needs to be pliable, then use a medium or lighter-weight paper and so on.

3. If you can afford it, buy separate brushes for different jobs to reduce the risk of getting old paint or glue where you don't want it. Always make sure you wash your brushes thoroughly after using any paint and especially after using craft glue.

folded books

FOLDED BOOKS, SOMETIMES CALLED CONCERTINAS, ACCORDIONS OR leporellos, originally developed from the scroll form. Scrolls were awkward to read because they had to be unwound and rewound continually in order to locate specific passages. By folding the length of cloth, paper or papyrus into a zigzag and forming pages, reading became a much simpler task. The folded book has been widely used in Japan and the Far East for many centuries, with some of the most beautiful and delicate examples being the 'flutter' books made from rice paper or other fine papers. Paper was not the only material used for making folded books. In India and Sumatra birch bark was very popular up until the end of the 1800s and even old stiffened clothes were folded up and used for making account books.

From simple concertina fold to the **more complex star structures described** later in this book, these forms are functional and fun.

They can be used in many ways: as notebooks, journals and albums; to make exciting greetings cards by adding illustrations and text; or as beautiful free-standing sculptural forms.

In this section you will learn the easy way to fold a perfect concertina, how to make books with and without glue and how to develop your own style by experimenting with unusual folds.

how to fold a concertina

THE EASIEST WAY TO FOLD THE PERFECT ZIGZAG IS ALWAYS TO BEGIN FOLDING INTO THE CENTRE, not from one end which may seem more obvious. First, decide how wide you want each fold to be and multiply this measurement by how many folds you want. Sticking to an even number of folds makes it easier to measure. A fold is a division of a length of paper with a crease down the centre. For example, if each fold is 10 cm (4 in) wide and you want four folds, then the total length of your paper should be 40 cm (16 in).

ONE FOLD

1 Fold the paper in half widthways (A). Then take one end (B) and fold it into the middle (A).

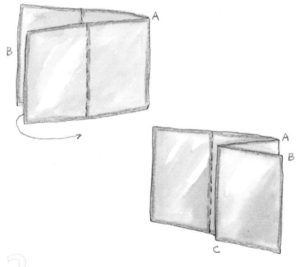

2 Fold the crease line at (C) back on itself and then match it up with the original fold line (A).

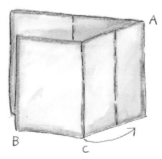

3 Then take the end (B) and fold up to crease (C). Repeat with the other half of the concertina.

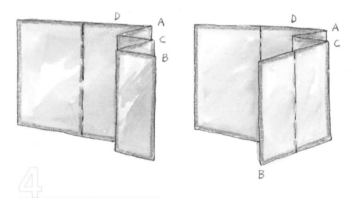

4 If your paper is not long enough to fold a concertina to the required size, you can extend it. To join two lengths, take two pieces of paper the size you need. On one, allow an extra 0.6 to 1 cm (¼ to ⅜ in) at one end. Crease along this point and fold over. Now fold both concertinas as described above. Then glue or paste the small hinge of paper and attach it to the back of the second fold (C).

pocket fold book

ADDING A FOLDED POCKET TO THIS ZIGZAG BOOK will give you extra space for collecting and storing small items. It works like a scrapbook, but because nothing is permanently glued, you can move the contents around or change them completely to suit your needs. You will need to use a fairly strong paper for the pockets to be useful, as they need to stand upright without sagging. The book is closed securely with ties.

MATERIALS

Paper for covering

Greyboard

Strong paper for the concertina fold

Ribbon, tape or cord for the ties

PVA glue

Wheatflour paste

Waxed and clean waste paper for pressing

EQUIPMENT

Knife and/or scalpel

Bone folder

Steel safety ruler

Dividers

Chisel, knife or bradawl

Hammer

Pressing boards and a weight

Glue brush

1

Decide how tall you want the concertina fold to be (A) and add the required pocket depth (B), making sure the grain direction runs head to tail. Fold up lengthways to form the pocket (C).

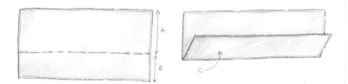

2

Fold up the concertina as described on page 24, keeping the pocket on the outside of the fold.

3

For the cover, cut two boards 3 mm (⅛ in) larger than the concertina fold on all four sides.

4

Cut two pieces of cover paper approximately 2 cm (¾ in) larger than the cover boards. Put waste paper under the boards and glue (stipple the glue to get a thin, even coat. See Glossary on page 11). Place the board down on the wrong side of the cover paper, turn it over and rub well with a bone folder or your hand through a piece of clean paper. If you have a press, nip the covered boards between pressing boards and waxed paper for a minute.

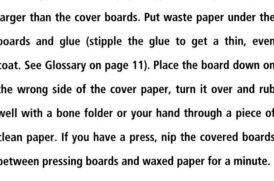

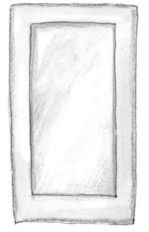

5

Use the dividers, or a ruler and a sharp pencil, to mark the turn-in allowance (A) 1.5 cm (⅝ in) out from the edge of the boards. Trim along these points with a scalpel and safety ruler (B).

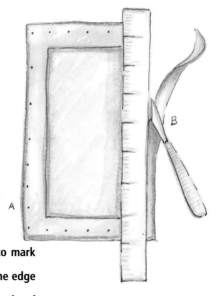

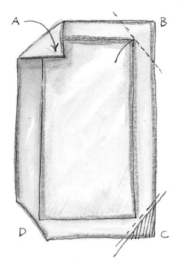

6

To cut the corners, first fold each paper corner over the board to form a right angle (A). Lift the corners up again; you now have a 45-degree crease line (B). Allow for the thickness of the board when cutting the corners. If you cut too close, the turn-ins will not meet when you turn them over. Therefore, measure the board thickness with the dividers (adding a bit extra) and transfer this measurement to the outside of the crease line, away from the board edge (C). Now cut along this line (D).

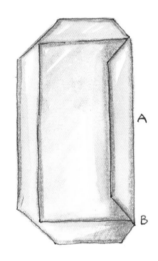

7

Glue one edge of the turn-in, making sure there is enough adhesive along the board edge. Then turn it over. Rub the paper down along the board edges first to stop any air bubbles forming. Then rub the turn-ins down well (A).

Notice that at either end of the turn-in, there is a small amount of cover paper overlapping the corner of the board (B). This needs to be flattened into the board edge with a bone folder or your thumb to avoid small 'ears' of paper forming and to obtain a neat finish. Do this at both ends, then repeat on the opposite side.

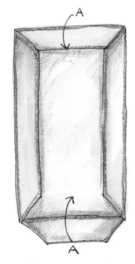

8

Finally glue down the remaining two turn-ins (A) and leave the boards to dry between clean paper and pressing boards under a weight.

9

To attach the ties you will need to make a slot in the front board using a hammer and chisel or a strong knife. To do this, you first have to find the halfway point of the board height and mark this point 2.5 cm (1 in) in from the board edge (A). Measure the width of your ribbon and transfer this measurement to the board taking point (A) as the centre of the line (B). Cut or chisel through the boards on to a pile of waste greyboards to avoid damaging the work surface.

10

To measure the ribbon length, first place the concertina fold between the two boards. Cut two lengths of ribbon, one four times the width and one twice the width of the board.

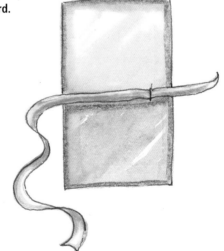

Remove the back board and the concertina and push the ribbon through the slit, keeping the longer piece on the left and the shorter one on the right. Glue down about 1 cm (⅜ in) of each end of the ribbon to the back of the board, on either side of the slit. Hammer flat.

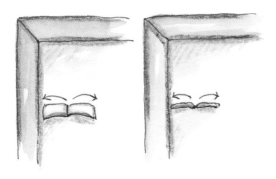

Place a piece of waste paper under the front fold of the concertina as protection and paste or glue the surface. Place this pasted side down on the inside of the front cover board, making sure it is central and the pocket fold is at the bottom (A). Repeat for the other side.

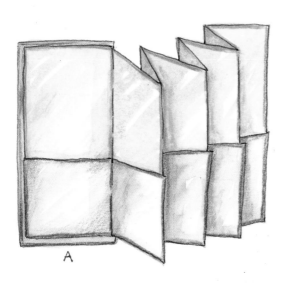

Open out the folded bottom pocket and pull the ribbons to the front to avoid making any indentations while the book is being pressed. Place waxed paper over the pasted boards and leave them to dry under a weight between paper and pressing boards.

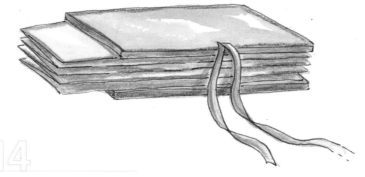

When the book is dry (leave overnight if possible), re-fold the bottom pocket and run a little glue along the edge at each end (A). Glue to secure the pocket fold.

To finish, take the longer ribbon around the back of the closed book and tie at the fore edge.

everlasting fold book

THE BEAUTY OF THIS BOOK IS ITS SIMPLICITY. There is very little to glue and the cover papers are wrapped around the boards. The concertina fold is slotted into the cover, so when one fold is full of notes, sketches or shopping lists, it can be removed and replaced with another. This book could be used as a diary or notebook, with the wrap-around cover making a handy place for keeping scraps and ephemera, such as wine labels and tickets, until they find a more permanent home. The fold can be as long as you like, but you may need to join sheets of paper together using the method described earlier.

MATERIALS

Cover paper—plain or decorative, medium-weight

Greyboard

Paper for the concertina fold

PVA glue

EQUIPMENT

Knife and/or scalpel

Steel safety ruler

Dividers

Set square

Cutting mat or board

Small glue brush

1 Fold a concertina to the required size, not too big to start with.

2 Using a knife and the safety ruler, cut two boards slightly larger than the folded concertina (A). Use a set square or the cutting mat grid to make sure the boards have right angles at each corner, and make sure the grain direction runs from top to bottom (B).

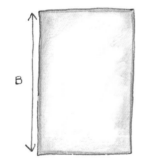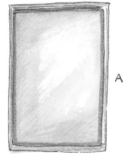

3 Cut two pieces of cover paper the same height as the boards (A) and twice the width (B), adding 1 cm (⅜ in) for an overlap (C).

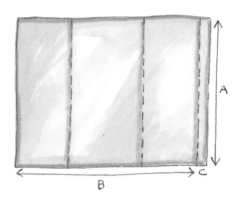

4 Wrap the paper round the boards, add a little glue along the edge of the narrower turn-in and overlap this with the wider one (A).

Cut a piece of cover paper for the spine. This should be the same height as the boards (A) and the same width as the concertina fold (B). Measure the width of the spine by creasing it around the folded pages (C) or by using dividers. Leave 2 cm (¾ in) of paper to each side of the creases; this will be attached to the boards.

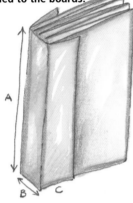

Run a little glue along the edge of the spine piece (A), line up one of the creased edges with the edge of the board and glue in place.

Place the concertina in position, run a little glue along the other edge of the spine piece, fold it around the book and place the second board exactly over the top of the first. Open the boards, take out the concertina and rub the glued areas down well.

Cut two pieces of cover paper, twice the length of the board (A) and the same width (B).

Wrap this cover paper lengthways round the boards, and tuck the overlap in at the head and tail (A & B). If you find it difficult to tuck in the overlap, cut it a little shorter.

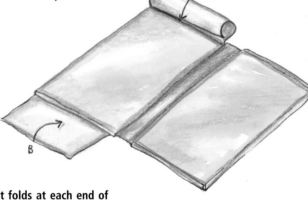

To complete the book, slot the last folds at each end of the concertina (A) into each edge of the inside cover (B).

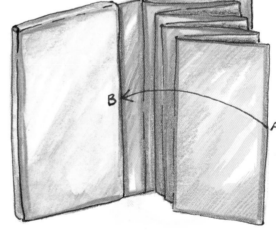

experimenting with folds

THE FOLLOWING DIAGRAMS AND ILLUSTRATIONS SHOW VARIATIONS ON THE BASIC CONCERTINA FOLD.

Using papers of different weights, try folding them and see how they behave. The thin, more fragile folds of the flutter book have a different quality from the slotted zigzag made of thin card. What happens if you fold the paper at an angle or slit one of the creases and fold in another direction? Different types of folding can be used to illustrate a poem or short story or to create a complex maze.

The best way to become familiar with your materials is by handling them, so try a few experimental folds of your own by doodling with some inexpensive paper.

FLUTTER BOOK

Using a very thin paper such as onion skin Japanese or bank paper, fold an extra-long zigzag. Join the folds as required and attach to a three-part board structure (described in the 'Fold-out Book' on pages 31-33). See also illustrated reference in the Gallery Section on pages 34-35.

SLOTTED ZIGZAG BOOK

Take two pieces of stiff paper or thin card cut to the same size. Score with a bone folder along the broken lines (see diagram) and make cuts half the height of the paper in the centre of each fold. Fold as a zigzag, turn one upside-down and slot together.

ALTERNATIVE FOLDS

Fold a flat piece of paper in half lengthways, then fold widthways into quarters. Open out the paper and make a slit down the middle, leaving the top fold intact (A). Fold the paper as a zigzag, starting at number one and ending at number eight.

If you fold the zigzags unevenly, you can sculpt any number of structures. You may need to shape the lower edge (B) if you want it to stand up.

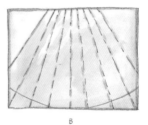

This fold is more complex (C) and the creases need to be measured and scored with a bone folder. Each crease line is folded both ways and then a little patience is needed to coax the folds into position. The solid and broken lines indicated show folds and reverse folds respectively.

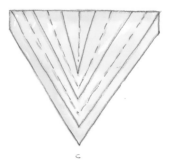

fold-out book

THIS BOOK IS INSPIRED BY A VELLUM FIFTEENTH-CENTURY DOCTOR'S NOTEBOOK and diagnostic chart in the British Library. Fold-outs are useful for maps, plans and charts and they could be an unusual way of displaying artwork. Instead of storing prints and drawings in a portfolio, why not fold them into pocket-sized bookworks?

MATERIALS

Paper or artwork for making the fold

Cover paper or bookcloth

Board lining paper (to complement cover paper and fold)

Greyboard

Scrap paper for making a pattern

Wheatflour paste

PVA glue

EQUIPMENT

Bone folder

Knife and/or scalpel

Steel safety ruler

Dividers

Cutting mat or board

Glue brush

Set square

Pressing boards and a weight

1

To work out the design of your folds, experiment with scrap paper first. When you have finalized your design, transfer the fold lines to the project paper and score with a bone folder. The more folds you want, the thinner the paper should be. Try to avoid folding the paper too many times as it may crease badly, especially at the corners.

2

In this example, the bottom left-hand section of the paper (A) will be pasted to the cover board. The vertical folds are made first (B) and then the zigzag is then folded in half (C).

A

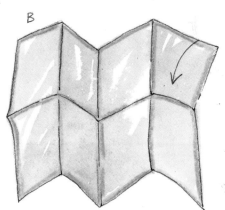
B

C

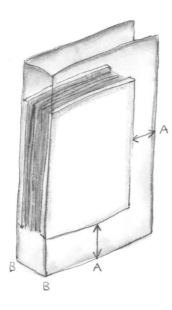

3

Measure and cut two boards 3 mm (⅛ in) bigger than the folded book on all four sides. Place the book inside the boards and use scrap paper folded round the boards to measure for the covering material. Cut the paper or cloth 2 cm (¾ in) larger than the boards all the way round (A) and crease along the board edges at the spine (B).

4

If the paper fold is 1 cm (⅜ in) thick or more, it is a good idea to add a spine lining to the cover for additional strength. The spine lining is often made from Kraft paper but most medium-weight papers will do. If the folded paper is really thick, you can use the same material as the cover boards. Cut a strip of lining paper the same height as the board and the same width as the paper fold down the spine. Put to one side.

5

Glue one board to the covering material with PVA glue and rub it down well. Place the book fold centrally on the glued board.

6

Glue the second board and place it, glued side up, over the top of the first board. Holding the board with the tips of your fingers, bring the cloth over the top, making sure it fits tightly at the spine.

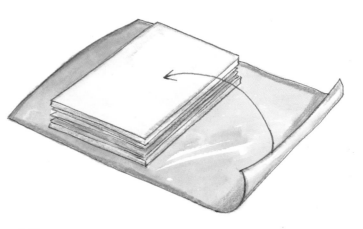

7

Before rubbing down, drop the board back and use a ruler to check that the boards are level. Work quickly before the glue dries, in case you need to move the board slightly to straighten it. Glue the spine lining paper and place it centrally between the two boards. Rub down well.

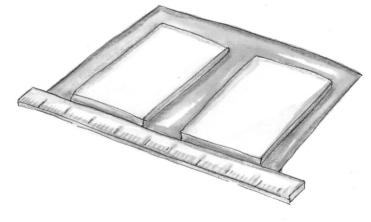

Fold, measure and cut the corners of the covering material (see page 26). Glue the turn-ins over the board edges and across the spine lining, rubbing down well between the boards into the joint (A). Remember to flatten the overlapping paper at the corners before turning in the adjacent edges. Leave to dry between clean paper and pressing boards under a weight.

A   A

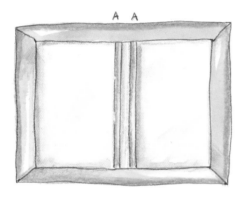

Cut a piece of your chosen lining paper, 3 mm (⅛ in) smaller than the cover on all four sides.

Paste the paper, and starting at one end, stick to the inside of the boards. Make sure that the paper fits snugly into the central joint or the cover will not open properly. Leave to dry flat as described previously.

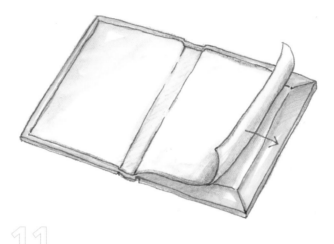

Paste the top folded section ((A) in step 2) of the book and attach centrally to the back cover board. Place a piece of waxed paper over this fold and close the book. Leave to dry overnight (or until the paste is completely dry) between pressing boards under a weight.

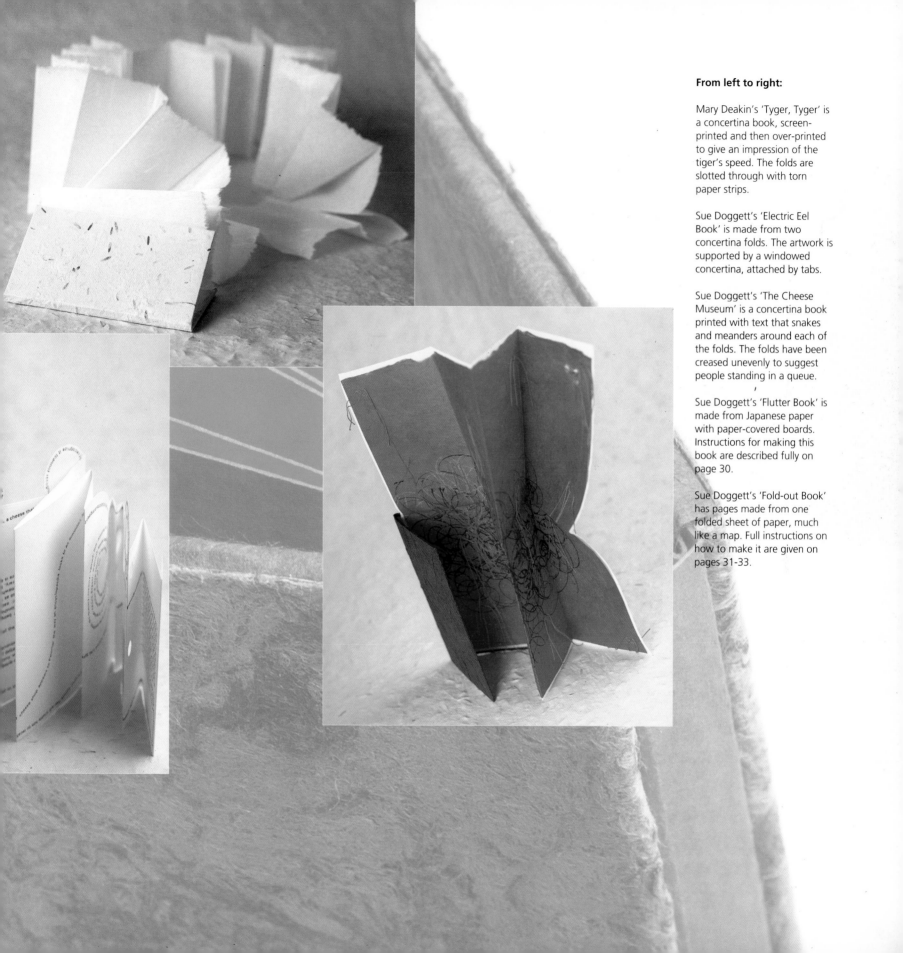

From left to right:

Mary Deakin's 'Tyger, Tyger' is a concertina book, screen-printed and then over-printed to give an impression of the tiger's speed. The folds are slotted through with torn paper strips.

Sue Doggett's 'Electric Eel Book' is made from two concertina folds. The artwork is supported by a windowed concertina, attached by tabs.

Sue Doggett's 'The Cheese Museum' is a concertina book printed with text that snakes and meanders around each of the folds. The folds have been creased unevenly to suggest people standing in a queue.

Sue Doggett's 'Flutter Book' is made from Japanese paper with paper-covered boards. Instructions for making this book are described fully on page 30.

Sue Doggett's 'Fold-out Book' has pages made from one folded sheet of paper, much like a map. Full instructions on how to make it are given on pages 31-33.

pamphlet sewing

PAMPHLET STITCH, ONE OF THE SIMPLEST METHODS OF SEWING, is based around three holes. The thread can be hidden, illustrated in the wrap-around book on the following pages, or visible as part of the design.

Pamphlet bindings can be fastened together **with coloured sewing thread,** cord, ribbon, raffia and even shoelaces.

If you want to make a larger book, increase the number of sewing holes to five, seven or more, or add an extra section to give you more pages and introduce a folded cover with a pleat. If you want to keep the structure really simple, the cover need only consist of two or three folds of paper with the sewing reduced to one central hole, a perfect way to make elegant personalized greetings cards.

To make a basic card or booklet, take one or two folds of your chosen paper and make a hole halfway. Then take a piece of matching or contrasting cord or ribbon and thread it through the hole from the outside. Take the ribbon over the top of the folds and finish off by going back through the central hole and round the bottom so that both ends of the ribbon are on the outside. Tie a bow to secure it and trim the ends at an angle to stop them from fraying.

wrap-around book

THIS SIMPLY SEWN BOOK HAS AN EXTENDED COVER which adds strength without weight. Try using a decorative paper with contrasting endpapers, or perhaps hand-made paper and coloured pages. The cover can contain a hidden message or secret artwork which can be seen only when it is fully open.

MATERIALS
Cover paper
Paper for endpapers
Paper for pages
Sewing thread

EQUIPMENT
Knife and/or scalpel
Steel safety ruler
Needle
Dividers
Bodkin bradawl or handled needle
Cutting mat

1

Divide the page paper in half to make folds. You will need about six folds of a medium-weight typing paper, or slightly thinner paper if you want extra pages.

2

Cut two folds of coloured or decorative paper for endpapers the same size as the page folds. Wrap these round the book.

3

If you want to make the fore edge neater, trim it now with a scalpel and safety ruler.

4

Cut a piece of cover paper the same height and five times the width of a page. Fold one end round the back of the book (A).

A

5

To prepare for sewing, take a piece of waste paper the same height as the book and divide it into four. The easiest way to do this is to fold the paper in half widthways, open it up and then fold each end into the middle and line up with the centre crease.

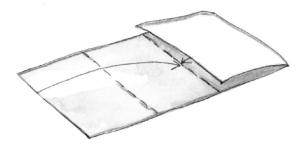

6

Fold the paper in half lengthways and place it in the centre fold of the book. Mark the sewing points where the fold lines intersect. This will be your sewing pattern or guide to follow.

7

From inside, push the needle through the centre fold of the book at the three points, making sure the needle comes out exactly on the fold of the cover paper. Remove the paper sewing pattern out of the centre of the book.

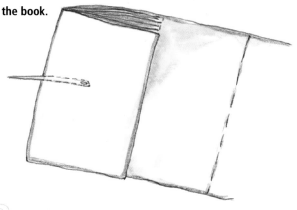

8

Sew the book as follows: From the inside, take the thread through the centre hole so it is now on the outside (A). Next, sew through one of the other holes going back into the centre (B). Bring the needle out again at the last hole (C). To finish, go back through the centre hole, tighten the sewing and, making sure there is a thread on each side of the long stitch, tie a double knot. Cut off the excess thread to about 1 cm ($^3/_8$ in) and close the book. Here the knot appears in the middle of the book. If you don't want the knot to show, begin sewing from the outside.

9

Fold the cover paper back on itself, creasing at the fore edge of the book (A). Then take the paper round the spine and back towards the fore edge and crease again.

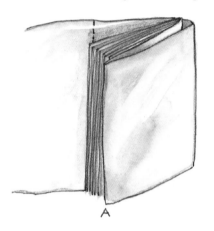

A

10

Cut a tab from the remaining fifth of the cover paper as shown in the diagram. The distance (A) is half the width of a page. (B) is approximately a third of the book's height but you can make it bigger or smaller as desired.

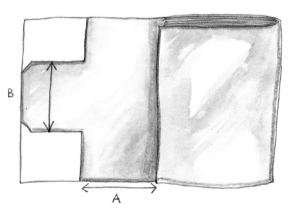

B

A

11

Lay the tab over the inside cover and make a pencil mark on each side of its width.

12

Unfold the cover completely, put a spare piece of board or a cutting mat under the book and cut a slit between the two pencil marks.

13

Re-fold the cover around the book and insert the tab into the slit. Trim the head and tail of the book with a scalpel to even up the edges if required.

double pamphlet fold with ties

THIS NOTEBOOK IS ALSO SEWN THROUGH THREE HOLES, but an extra section has been added to make more pages. The cover is made from two sheets of paper with a zigzag fold in the centre, through which the two sections are attached. The ties are glued between the zigzag fold before sewing and can wrap around the book as many times as you like. You can also make this book without ties, using a coloured thread which contrasts with the cover papers, or one which blends to become invisible. Either way, the spine will appear simple and elegant.

1

Fold two sections as in the previous project.

2

Cut another fold of paper for the inner cover. This needs to be the same height as the sections made above and the same width as an opened-out page fold. Add 4 cm (1½ in) for the zigzag (A). Do the same with the cover paper.

3

Fold both sheets in half and place one inside the other. Measure 2 cm (¾ in) in from the folded edge. Place a ruler along the measured line (A) and score with a bone folder.

Make a sewing pattern on a piece of waste paper as described in the previous project, 'Wrap-around Book'.

5

If you want to add ties to your book, cut each one to the required length (at least one-and-a-half times the book width) and attach them inside the zigzag of the cover folds with a little PVA glue. The ties should not interfere with the sewing so use your sewing pattern as a guide to avoid these points.

Take both folded sections, place them either side of the cover folds and mark for sewing (A). The sewing holes should go through the folds of both sections and cover papers (B) at the same time.

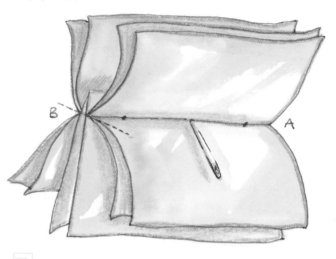

Sew as in the previous project and finish off with a double knot. Close the book by bringing the covers round to meet the fore edges of the two sections.

five-, seven- and nine-hole sewing

IF YOU WANT TO MAKE A LARGER book, you may need extra sewing points for strength.
Five- and seven-hole sewing is no more complicated than the three-hole method.

METHOD

It works like a figure-of-eight (see below, left). The thing to remember is that you must have one long stitch across the central hole, around which you tie the loose threads, and an odd number of holes. Apart from these rules, you can sew with as many holes as you like.

If you place the knot on the outside of the book, it can become the starting point for a design, the simplest example being one-hole ribbon sewing. If you tie a knot instead of a bow and extend the ribbons, you can use them to make ties or tassels, or you can cut slits in the cover paper and thread the ribbon through. The sewing thread or cord can be sewn, knotted or tied to other materials such as twisted silk, beads and tassels, all of which can turn this simple but versatile book form into something special. See the Gallery Section for some examples of this decorative sewing.

From left to right:

Clare Bryan's 'Forbidden Fruit' is a pamphlet stitch book with text and images printed on a variety of papers and tissues, protected within thin wooden boards and a bookcloth spine.

Emma Ruffle and Sue Doggett's 'Pamphlets' use simple three-hole pamphlet stitching and bark papers, Japanese tissue and watercolour papers.

Sue Doggett's 'Serpents and Skulls' are two small pamphlet stitch books containing printed text and images. They are housed in a simple case which is made like a photograph frame and kept in place by two strips of ribbon.

Emma Ruffle's pamphlet bindings are sewn with frayed string and natural materials as design elements.

Sue Doggett's 'Pamphlets' have three-, five- and seven-hole stitching with additional beads and extended threads forming tassels. These formats are described earlier in the chapter, on page 43.

multi-section sewing

IF YOU WANT TO MAKE A LARGER BOOK, you will need to add more sections to make a multi-section book, or codex. The word codex comes from the Latin *caudex*, meaning 'trunk of a tree', and refers to the method used by the Romans to hinge their wooden, wax-filled writing tablets together. From its beginnings as an early type of ring binder, the codex developed into the familiar form we call a book today.

To function as a book, the sections need to be sewn together. Adding sewing supports such as tapes or cords not only makes the structure stronger but also adds visual interest.

This section is divided into two parts. First, all the sewing techniques are described; then, illustrated examples show methods of attaching boards and covers, giving you the opportunity to mix sewing and binding styles to create the book you want.

Sewing is one of the most important structural elements of a book, and it needs to be strong and secure if the book is to be used regularly.

Remember to keep the tension even by constantly tightening up the threads. The best way to do this is to tighten each row of sewing as you go along. If the sewing is loose or uneven, the sections may twist around when the book is being used. This puts a strain on the sewing and could cause the paper to tear.

sewing on tapes

TAPES ARE ADDED TO STRENGTHEN the spine and provide decoration. Before sewing, prepare your sections. A good size to start with is probably 15 x 20 cm (6 x 8 in), which would make a useful notebook. Fold the paper into about eight sections, allowing three to four folds for each. For more pages in your book, add more pages per section and use a thinner paper. Press them between boards under a weight for a few hours or overnight if you have time. You can leave the torn edges as they are or you can trim all the sections to the same size before sewing.

MATERIALS

Paper for sections

Linen sewing thread and/or coloured threads and silks

Cotton tape, ribbon, cords, thongs etc., for sewing supports

Beeswax

Scrap paper

EQUIPMENT

Sewing needles

Pencil

Pressing board

Masking tape

Bodkin or handled needle

1

Make the sections square at one end and across the spine. Place them on top of a pressing board.

2

Decide how many tapes you require. For instance, a small book like this could have three or four tapes, while a larger book would probably have more. It also depends on the width of the tape or ribbon, so you might use more thin tapes or fewer thick ones.

3

Tapes should be long enough to cover the spine of the book with overhang of about 6 to 8 cm (2½ to 3 in). They need to be longer if they are being used for decorative lacing or tying.

4

Make a pencil mark 1 to 1.5 cm (⅜ to ⅝ in) in from either end of the book where the kettlestitches will be. Divide the space between the kettlestitch points according to the number of tapes being used. Mark with a pencil. The examples below show measuring up for three tapes or four tapes.

2 TAPES

4 TAPES

5

Place the tapes centrally over the pencil marks and secure with masking tape on the edge of the pressing board.

6

Make a sewing pattern using a folded piece of paper the same length as the sections. Line up the folded edge with the book and mark a point at each end where the kettlestitches are, and mark two points, either side of each tape.

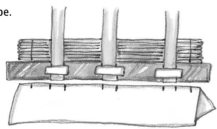

7

Place the pattern in the centre of each section and carefully pierce the sewing holes. Make sure the needle comes out exactly on the fold and not on either side of it.

8

Place the first section on the pressing board, lining up the sewing holes with the tapes. Begin at (A). Take the needle into the centre of the first section, then out again at (B), next to the tape. Sew across the tape and go back in through the next hole (C). Continue up to the end hole.

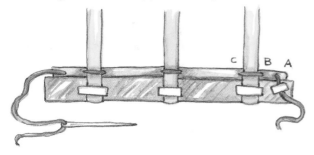

9

Place the second section on top of the first, taking the needle through the end hole. Continue sewing as before. Repeat for the third section.

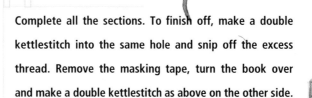

10

To form the kettlestitch, take the needle to the section below and behind the linking stitch (A). Pull the thread to form a loop, take the needle through the loop, pointing up, and pull tight. Make a kettlestitch at each end of each section, always going down to the section below the one you have just sewn.

11

Complete all the sections. To finish off, make a double kettlestitch into the same hole and snip off the excess thread. Remove the masking tape, turn the book over and make a double kettlestitch as above on the other side.

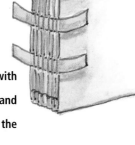

12

Remove the pressing board. Close the sewing holes with a needle point to neaten the spine. Add endpapers and attach boards or make a case binding following the directions on pages 56–57 or 62–65.

sewing over cords or thongs

BOOKS WERE TRADITIONALLY SEWN ON TO CORDS OR THONGS, which were covered with leather and appeared as raised bands along the spine. Cord sewing follows the same principles as tape sewing, except you only make one hole per cord. When you sew, the needle goes back into the same hole it came out so the cord is looped. Select your materials from the list on page 48.

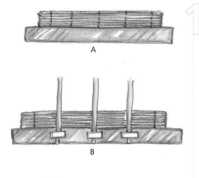

1 Place the sections on a pressing board. Mark the sections and sewing pattern as in figure (A) and put cords in position. Secure them with masking tape (B). The method of sewing and adding sections is the same as for tapes, except at sewing points (C), where the cord is looped. Because of this looping it is necessary to tighten the thread at each cord rather than at the end of each section.

2 To wrap the cord with extra thread, come out of the sewing hole and wind it round the cord as many times as you need (probably two or three times depending on the thickness of the thread) before going back into the section through the same hole. Be careful not to wind round the cord too many times or the sections will not lie flat.

3 Finish off as before, with a double kettlestitch.

joining a new thread

IF YOU ARE SEWING MORE THAN three or four sections, you will probably need to join on a new thread at some point. The best way to do this is to make a 'weaver's knot', which is very secure and can be positioned exactly. You can join the thread on the inside or the outside of the book but if your sewing is going to show then the knot is best hidden inside. Try to avoid joining at the kettlestitch as this may weaken the sewing.

1 Make two loops in the new thread.

2 Take the right-hand loop through the left-hand loop.

3 Tighten the left-hand loop but not completely.

4 Take the old thread through the large loop of the new thread (C) until it is tight around the old thread (B), pull the two ends of the new thread tightly (A). The old thread should 'snap' through the loop. Trim the loose ends to about 1 cm (⅜ in).

longstitch bindings

IN A LONGSTITCH BINDING, THE SECTIONS AND COVER ARE SEWN SIMULTANEOUSLY, so the sewing becomes part of the design. The longstitches on the spine can be treated in a number of ways, but traditionally they have been wrapped and plaited. You can add beading, silk or metallic threads and knotting to the stitches as you are sewing, or you can work on them afterwards by pinching them together and using embroidery stitches. You can also vary the length and number of stitches you use. Select your materials from the list on page 48.

If you are using paper for the cover, it is a good idea to strengthen the spine fold by gluing on a strip of linen before making the sewing holes. This will stop the paper from tearing and extend the life of the book.

1 Cut, fold and press sections ready for sewing. Trim to the required size.

2 Cut a piece of scrap paper big enough to wrap loosely round the sections. Add an extra 3 cm (1¼ in) all round (A). Crease along each side of the backbone of the book to form the spine allowance.

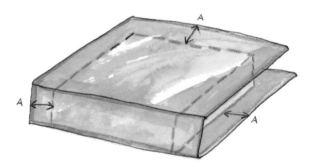

3 Use this pattern to cut your cover paper. Transfer the spine allowance to the cover paper and crease. Allow 3 mm (⅛ in) extra to form the 'square', and 3 cm (1¼ in) for the 'turn-ins' (see Glossary on page 11 for an explanation of these terms). Score and crease.

4 Mark and pierce the sewing holes in the cover paper. Divide the distance between (A) and (B) into seven equal parts. This will give you six equally spaced sewing points. Pierce the paper at these points and then pierce holes horizontally across the spine, making a sewing hole for each section. Continue for each of the six sewing points.

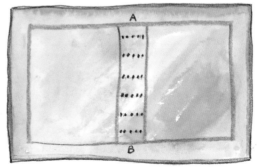

5

For clarity the turn-in allowance does not show on the diagrams. Begin sewing from inside the first section, coming out through the cover at the second hole from the end (A). Sew running stitches in and out of the cover and the section until you come to the end (B).

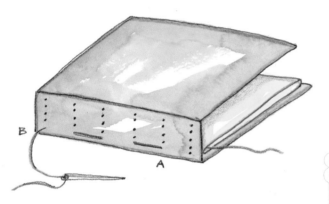

6

Add the second section. Take the needle through the end hole immediately above and continue sewing as before.

7

Proceed until all the sections have been sewn.

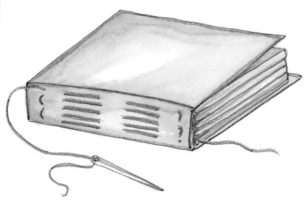

8

Then go back, filling in all the missing stitches at the head and tail. Apart from the first and last sections, all other longstitches will have double threads on the spine. You should end up back inside the first section at an end hole. Knot the two loose thread ends together and trim.

9

Turn the cover in as described on page 68-69.

japanese-style sewing

TRADITIONAL JAPANESE BINDINGS USE A STAB STITCH to bind the pages and cover together. The simplest and most elegant stitch is the four-hole or 'Yotsume Toji' binding. You can use any paper in single sheets for this book but why not try the traditional method of sewing with the folds at the fore edge? You could use a thin, delicate paper for the pages, with a rich, decorative cover chosen from the many gorgeous Japanese papers available. The sewing thread could be a contrasting colour, either rich and silky or delicate and understated, but it needs to be thick enough to enhance the beauty and simplicity of the sewing pattern.

The instructions here are for a limp paper cover. Select your materials from the list on page 48.

1

Fold the paper for the sections and make them square. Cut two pieces of decorative cover paper. Place one on each side of the book block. If you wish, trim the spine edge of the book before sewing.

2

Put a weight on the text block while you make the sewing holes. Lightly score a line 2 cm (¾ in) in from the spine edge (A). Measure 2 cm (¾ in) in from the head and tail (B). Divide the space between these two points into three, which will give you the remaining two sewing points (C). At these points, make a hole through the covers and pages using a bodkin, or needle, depending on the thickness your book is going to be.

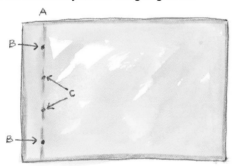

3

Start sewing through the spine, a few pages down from the top of the book, and come up through hole (A). Leave enough thread to tie later.

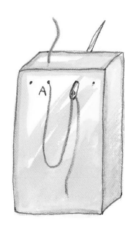

4

Continue sewing as shown in the diagrams.

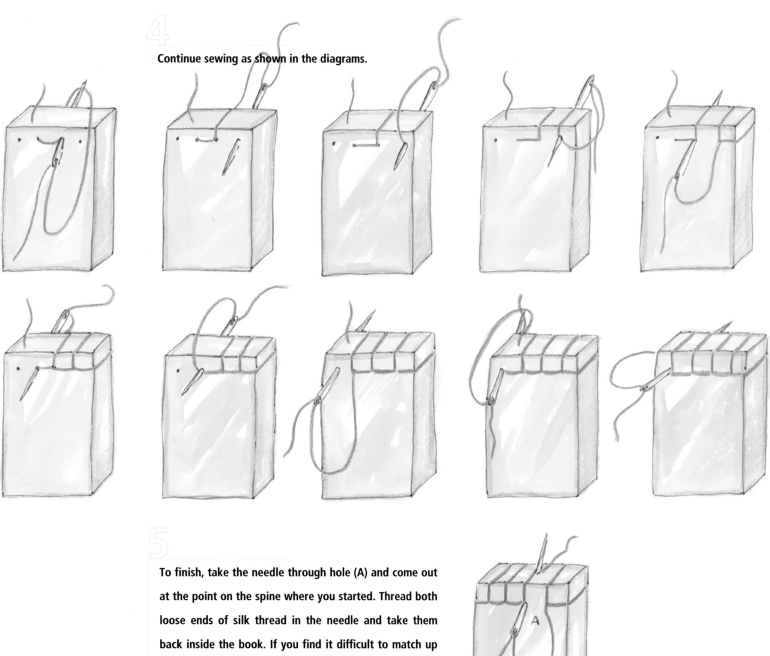

5

To finish, take the needle through hole (A) and come out at the point on the spine where you started. Thread both loose ends of silk thread in the needle and take them back inside the book. If you find it difficult to match up the threads, take the needle right up through hole (A) to the spine of the book. It may be easier to find the original sewing entrance by going back into hole (A) from here.

BACK

6

Open up the book and tie the two ends together. Trim and dab on a little glue. Close the book.

other stab stitches

IN ADDITION TO THE DECORATIVE JAPANESE SEWING described here, there are other simple forms of stab stitch that you can turn into fantastic and exotic creations.

The simplest method is to sew a continuous running stitch. Winding a coloured thread through each stitch creates a whipped running stitch (A). You can oversew the spine, using very large or very small stitches, experiment with cross stitch (B). Try using single threads and knotting through the holes and at the spine (C). You can add tassels, beads or driftwood and, by extending the sewing, you can create all manner of ties and wrappings (D). There really is no limit to the variations possible with this simple format.

A

B

D

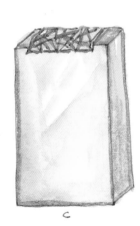

C

attaching covers and

boards

THERE ARE LOTS OF WAYS YOU CAN put covers on your books once they have been sewn. In some of the sewing methods described in the previous chapter, such as the Japanese and longstitch books, the covers are attached at the time of sewing. However, the remainder of the stitches and board attachments are interchangeable, giving you the freedom to experiment with your own materials and ideas.

Tapes and cords can be glued, nailed or sewn on to the cover boards using a variety of decorative techniques and stitches.

If you don't want the tapes to show or be part of the design, glue them between two precovered boards. Another way of attaching tapes and cords to boards is the traditional method of lacing in. This involves cutting slots or holes in the cover boards through which the sewing supports are laced. Recesses can be cut into the boards if you want the tapes or cords to lie flat. Originally, the book would have been covered after lacing, but with the exposed sewing method, the boards are usually covered first.

In addition, there are two specific projects to give you even more choice. These two books are very different in construction. One is a hardback book with pasted endpapers and the other is a limp paper binding that requires no adhesive at all. You can use any type of paper for covering boards but remember, the softer and more delicate the paper, the more it will wear. If you want a really tough book, use bookbinding cloth.

attaching endpapers (tipping on)

MATERIALS

Coloured or decorative
paper for endpapers

Waste paper

EQUIPMENT

Knife and/or scalpel

Steel safety ruler

PVA glue

Glue brush

Pressing boards and
a weight

1 Cut two pieces of your chosen endpaper and fold them in two, so that they are the same size as the pages of your book. Lay out some waste paper and place the endpapers down one on top of the other, with the folded edges about 5 mm (³/₁₆ in) away from each other. Lay a piece of waste paper 5 mm (³/₁₆ in) away from the top fold. Using PVA glue, glue the exposed folds, brushing out to avoid getting glue underneath. Remove the waste paper and throw it away immediately.

2 Lay the book on its side, folding back the tapes. Place the glued edge of one endpaper on the top section so that the folded edge is lined up exactly with the edge of the backbone. Rub down, then turn over and repeat with the second endpaper. Leave to dry between pressing boards under a weight. In this exposed sewing style of binding the spine is not glued, so now move on to the boards.

fill-ins

IF YOU WANT A REALLY SMOOTH, STYLISH FINISH on the inside of the cover boards, you can line them with paper before putting down the endpaper.

MATERIALS

Lining paper

PVA glue

Waxed paper

Fine sandpaper

EQUIPMENT

Knife and/or scalpel

Steel safety ruler

Cutting mat or board

Glue brush

Pressing boards and a
weight

1 Cut two pieces of paper the same thickness as the cover paper to fit between the turn-ins on the inside of the cover boards. Make sure the grain direction runs from head to tail.

2 Coat the paper with glue and stick it down. Close the board, turn it over, and repeat on the board on the other side. Put waxed paper over the glued paper and leave to dry between pressing boards under a weight.

3 When the fill-in is dry, using a fine sandpaper, you can gently sand over the tapes, cords etc., until the surface is smooth. Put in the endpapers as described previously.

cutting recesses

1

Cut your cover boards to the required size, adding 3 mm (⅛ in) at the head, tail and fore edge. Decide how long you want the tapes to be, then cut them to the desired length.

2

Place the boards on the book and the tapes in position, then mark the width and length of the tapes on the boards with a pair of dividers. Remove the board.

3

Using a scalpel and safety ruler, cut and peel away the area of board between the divider points to the depth of the tape.

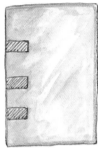

4

Coat the boards with PVA glue and cover with paper or cloth, making sure the covering material is pushed down well into the recesses. Fold, cut and glue down the corners and turn-ins as described on pages 25–26 and leave the covered boards between waxed paper and pressing boards under a weight to dry.

MATERIALS

Cover boards
Waxed paper
PVA glue

EQUIPMENT

Knife and/or scalpel
Steel safety ruler
Cutting mat or board
Dividers
Glue brush
Pressing boards and a weight

attaching boards

1

Use the equipment listed on page 60. Place the covered boards in position on the book and position the tapes over the recesses. Mark with divider points where the sewing holes are to be.

2

Remove the boards and make holes using a bodkin or small drill. Remember to use a pile of waste boards when hammering or drilling through a cover board so you don't damage the work surface.

3

Coat the recesses with a little PVA glue and stick down the tapes. Turn over and repeat with the other side. Leave to dry between pressing boards.

4

Using your chosen sewing pattern, sew over the tapes and through the boards, knotting and gluing the thread on the inside.

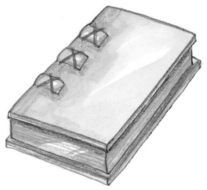

5

You can either paste down the endpapers, or paste in a lining paper on the inside of the board.

i) To paste down the endpapers, put a piece of waste paper between the endpapers and paste them, brushing out from the centre. Remove the waste paper and position the board squarely over the paste down (see Glossary on page 11). Turn over and repeat with the other side of the book. Place some waxed or blotting paper between the pasted endpapers and leave the book to dry thoroughly between clean paper and pressing boards under a weight.

ii) To line the boards, cut two pieces of decorative or plain lining paper 3 mm ($\frac{1}{8}$ in) smaller than the board on all four sides. Apply paste and place squarely over the inside of the board. Turn over and repeat on the other side of the book.

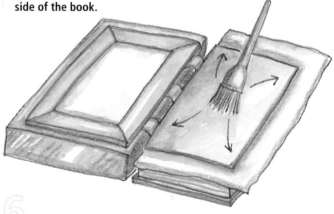

6

Leave the book to dry as described in 5i and the book is now complete.

lacing-in boards

IF YOU NEED A STRONGER CONSTRUCTION for your book, or you want to slot the tapes or cords in and out of the boards as part of the design, you must pierce the boards as well as cut recesses.

1 Attach endpapers and cut boards to size as described previously. Decide how much of the tape or cord you want showing on the cover board. Measure but don't cut yet. Cut recesses to this measurement and cover the boards following steps 1 to 4 of 'Attaching Boards'.

2 Using a chisel or bradawl, make a slit or hole at the end of each recess, where the tape or cord will go through.

3 Turn the boards over and cut recesses on the inside, extending about 2 cm (¾ in) beyond the slits. If you want to weave the tapes or cords in and out of the boards, make slits and recesses accordingly.

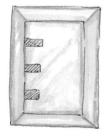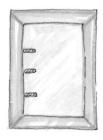

4 Place one board in position on the book. Coat the recesses with glue, making sure a small amount goes into the slits or holes, and thread the tapes or cords through.

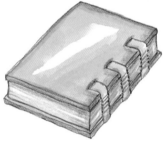

5 Drop the cover board back on to a pile of pressing boards. Cut the tapes or cords to fit into the recesses, glue in place and hammer flat. Turn over and repeat on the other side of the book.

6 Put down the endpapers or lining papers as described previously and leave them to dry overnight as indicated earlier.

MATERIALS
PVA glue
EQUIPMENT
Chisel or bradawl
Knife and/or scalpel
Glue brush
Pressing boards and a weight
Hammer

case binding

THIS STYLE OF BINDING IS THE ONE we are most familiar with – the commercial hardback book. The hard cover is referred to as a case, hence the term 'case binding'. It is more hard-wearing than some of the more decorative structures, because the sewing is protected by spine linings and a greyboard cover. It is suitable for most uses, but especially for notebooks and sketchbooks. Check that the grain direction of all your materials runs from head to tail, especially the endpapers, or they will stretch the wrong way and buckle when pasted.

MATERIALS

Greyboard

Cover paper or cloth

Coloured or decorative paper for endpapers

Paper for pages

Sewing thread

Mull

Kraft paper

PVA glue

Wheatflour paste

Waxed paper for pressing

EQUIPMENT

Knife and/or scalpel

Steel safety ruler

Needle

Dividers

Cutting mat or board

Glue brushes

Set square

Pressing boards

1 Sew sections on to tapes as described in 'Sewing on Tapes', on pages 48–49 and add endpapers as described in 'Attaching Endpapers', on page 58.

2 Leaving the tapes out, put the book between pressing boards and place a weight on top. Place glue along the spine, making sure you have enough glue between each of the sections by rubbing the glue in with your finger. Leave to dry.

3 If you have access to a guillotine or paper cutter with a clamp and want to trim your book, do so now.

4 Cut a piece of mull slightly shorter than the book at each end, and 3 to 4 cm (1¼ to 1½ in) wider than the spine on each side. Glue the mull to the spine of the book. Do not glue the excess, this will be pasted down with the tapes later.

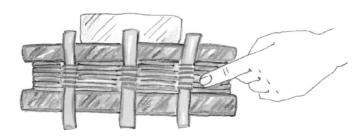

5

Cut two strips of kraft paper the same width as the spine, one piece to fit underneath the tapes (A) and the other to run the full length (B). Glue the small pieces to the spine first, then the full strip, and rub down well with a bone folder. If your book is large or thick, you can add an extra lining of kraft paper.

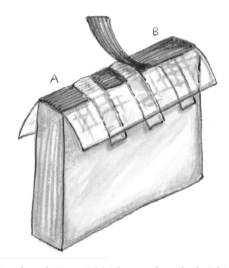

6

Cut two boards 6 mm (¼ in) longer than the height of the book and 1 mm (¹⁄₁₆ in) narrower than the width. Push the board out by 3 mm (⅛ in) at the fore edge, giving a 5 mm (³⁄₁₆ in) joint allowance. This allowance is very important – without it, the book won't open properly.

7

Place the boards in position on each side of the book and squeeze together. Measure the combined thickness of the book and both boards with dividers to determine the width of the spine board.

Note: Don't measure at the backbone. The tapes and sewing make it thicker than the rest of the book. Cut a piece of board this width and the same height as the cover boards.

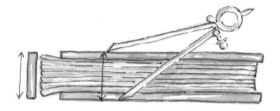

8

Cut a piece of paper or cloth 2 cm (¾ in) bigger on all sides than the area of the boards and spine as laid out in the diagram. Leave more cloth or paper than you need; you can always trim it down later. Coat one board with glue and stick it down. Turn over and rub down well.

9

The joint allowance is 5 mm (³/₁₆ in), but you need to add a board thickness to this. Although you are gluing the spine piece down flat, when the cover is closed, it will stand on its side (A).

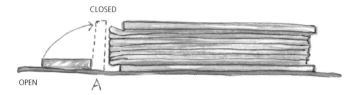

CLOSED

OPEN   A

10

Set the dividers to this measurement and mark out from the edge of the glued board. Lay a ruler along the base of the board and glue the spine piece. Place in position, lining up the divider points with the edge of the spine piece, making sure that everything is level. Rub down.

A

11

Use the same allowance and technique to position the second board. Glue into position and rub down. Set the dividers to 1.5 cm (⁵/₈ in) for the turn-in and, using a scalpel and safety ruler, trim the excess paper or cloth.

12

Fold, crease and cut the corners, then glue down the turn-ins as described on pages 25–26. Leave to dry under a weight between waxed paper and pressing boards.

13

Trim back the mull and tapes to about 2.5 cm (1 in) using waste board to protect your book.

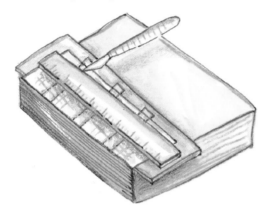

14

Place the book inside the case leaving an equal square all round, and pushing the book right into the spine. Lay it down flat and let the cover drop back. Put waste paper between the book and the endpaper, paste down the tapes and then paste the whole of the endpaper, including the mull. Brush the paste from the centre of the endpaper out to avoid getting paste under the endpaper. Carefully remove the waste sheet.

15

Without dislodging the book, bring the cover over, pushing the spine into the backbone of the book. Drop the cover down on to the paste down (see Glossary on page 11). Don't be tempted to open the board out flat once it is pasted, because the endpaper is wet and will stretch, causing creases when you shut the book again. Turn the book over and repeat on the other side.

16

Put waxed or blotting paper between the endpapers and wrap the book in clean waste paper. Place a pressing board on each side of the book as far up as the joint so the spine protrudes. Put the book in a press if you have one, or under a heavy weight. Leave the book to dry completely before use, preferably overnight. Don't use the book or leave it unweighted while the endpapers are still wet, or the boards will not dry flat.

limp paper binding
with slotted spine

THIS BOOK IS SEWN ON TO TAPES, RIBBONS OR PAPER STRIPS that are slotted through a paper cover. There is no gluing involved, so everything is held together by folding. Once you have mastered the sewing, the rest is easy. Choose a strong, hard-wearing paper such as a hand-made plant fibre or Khadi paper as illustrated in the Gallery Section. The sewing supports and slotted spine strip can be made from the same paper or in a contrasting colour for dramatic effect. If you want something softer, you can use ribbons, which can be extended to become ties or wrappings.

MATERIALS
Strong paper for cover
Paper for pages
Ribbon, tape or paper for sewing supports
Sewing thread

EQUIPMENT
Knife and/or scalpel
Steel safety ruler
Bone folder
Dividers
Set square
Cutting mat or board
Needle

1 Sew up the book as described in 'Sewing on Tapes'.

2 Make a paper pattern for the cover. First take a sheet of paper large enough to wrap around the sewn sections with about 4.5 cm (1¾ in) extra all round.

3 Lay the book on the paper and draw round it (A). Then turn it over, marking the spine width (B). Drop the book down and draw round the other side.

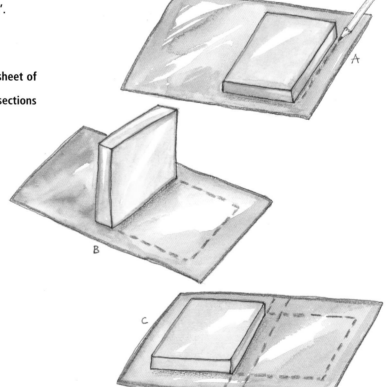

4

Transfer these marks to your cover paper. Extend the book edge measurements out by 3 mm (⅛ in). Score along these turn-ins and along the joints with a ruler and bone folder.

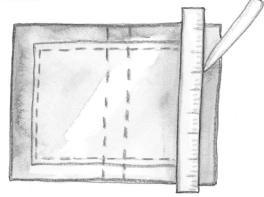

6

Extend a drawn line from these points across the spine and then cut through with a sharp scalpel.

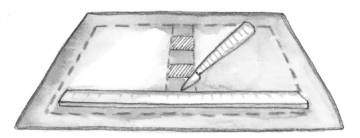

7

Cut along the spine fold between the slits and remove the paper. These holes should correspond with the position of the tapes on the book.

5

Lay the back of the book on the spine fold of the paper and, with the point of the dividers, mark the position of the tapes or ribbons.

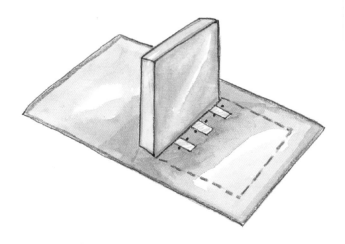

8

Measure 1 cm (⅜ in) from the top and bottom of each hole and mark with the point of the dividers (A). Cut through the cover vertically between these points (B).

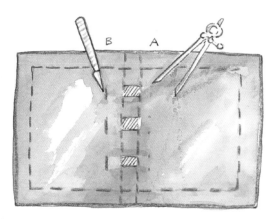

9

If you are extending ribbons to make ties, cut slits along the fore edge turn-ins where desired (A) or (B).

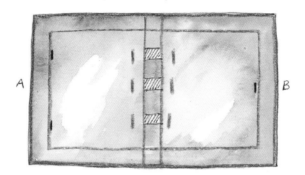

10

Cut the cover paper as in the diagram below.

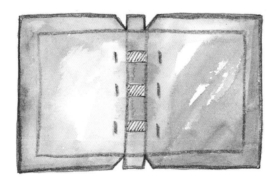

11

Cut the corners to form a tab, as shown below. The measurements are (A) = 6 mm (¼ in) and (B) = 12 mm (½ in).

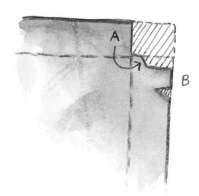

12

Fold all the turn-ins over along their precreased edges and mark each side of the tab with the dividers as shown.

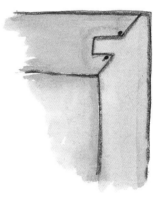

13

Open out the folded turn-ins and make a slit between the two divider points at each corner (A).

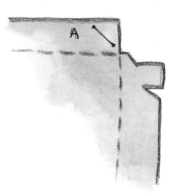

14

Cut a spine strip from the cover paper. It should be the same height as the cover and slightly narrower than the width of the spine. Lay the spine piece in position on the cover paper and turn in the smaller tabs at (A) and (B).

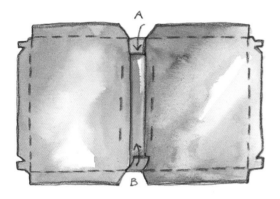

15

Lay the book over the cover spine, lining up the tapes with the slits. Push each tape through the corresponding slit at the spine fold.

16

When all the tapes are pulled through, take them back inside the cover through the remaining slits. Pull tight so that the back of the book fits snugly into the spine of the cover.

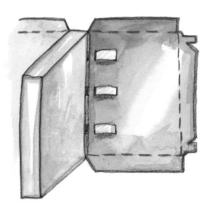

17

Fold the turn-ins around the first and last pages of the book (or the endpapers if you have attached them) and push the tabs through the slots at each corner.

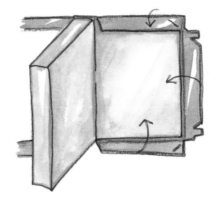

From left to right:

Vivien Frank's 'Bestiary' uses a binding sewn in the Coptic style with no tapes. The boards are made from laminated hand-made paper and the signatures are guarded with Japanese Mingei paper.

Sue Doggett's 'Stab stitch and Japanese Bindings' are made from hand-made paper and silk sewing thread.

Sue Doggett and Penny Stanford's hardcover books are three case bindings (see page 62). The images on the standing books are mono-printed and coloured with watercolour pencil. The cover of the book in the foreground is screen printed with text and imagery.

Sue Doggett and Vivien Frank's 'Longstitch Bindings' (see page 51).

variations on the fold

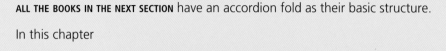

ALL THE BOOKS IN THE NEXT SECTION have an accordion fold as their basic structure.

In this chapter

there are all sorts of additions
to the zigzag, increasing even further the
creative possibilities of this
versatile and exciting form.

All the techniques used here have been described in detail in the previous chapter, and some of them have been developed into major projects later in the book. You don't have to stick rigidly to these instructions; you can mix and match many of the techniques to create your own formats.

Some of the bookworks use a combination of folding and sewing and a variety of materials, so why not try some of the paper-decorating techniques described in the first chapter? All of these structures are ideal for carrying text and artwork. Perhaps you could try simple monoprinting on to a long fold of paper and then folding it into a zigzag, or use text, photocopied or made from a collage, which could be added as extra sewn-in folds, or 'flags' perhaps. The Gallery Section has examples of all the book structures described in this chapter, with a few extras for inspiration.

concertinas with sewn folds

One way of extending the fold format is to add sewn sections. This way you can make a multi-section book where the concertina fold acts as a sewing support not unlike those in the previous chapters. Here, though, the support is expandable and sections can be sewn on both sides, making the format continuous. The fold of the zigzag can be narrow, like a fan fold so that the extra pages are extended, or the same size as the sections so that it works like an endpaper or cover. The former allows the pages to work as a continuous sequence with one section running into the next, while the latter breaks the sequence up.

Cover boards can be added to any of these format variations using the method described in the 'Pocket Fold Book'.

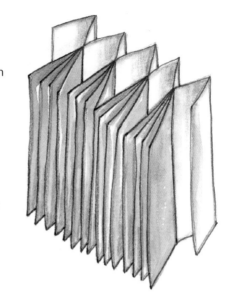

dos-à-dos

This binding is the simplest extension of the pamphlet and zigzag combination. The fold is extended by a half-fold and two sections are attached using the three-hole sewing method. Most structures can work in this back-to-back method, including the case binding, an example of which is illustrated in the Gallery Section at the end of this chapter.

Extended Dos-à-dos

Extend the length of the zigzag fold as much as you like and add the corresponding number of sections. This example has the sewing knot outside the folds where it has been augmented and used as a decorative feature.

uneven folds

Another way of altering the format is to fold the zigzag unevenly and attach sections of varying sizes. If you want the book to stand up, emphasizing its sculptural form, you need to make sure the foot of the book is level, which sometimes means having very odd-shaped folds.

extended sections

Make a fan fold and use the pamphlet stitch to sew sections to the fold edges. This format is a great way to display prints or artwork that you want to open completely flat. If you want the book to open conventionally and have a stable spine, you can sew the concertina to sewing supports after sewing in the pages (see 'Multi-section Sewing').

Random Sections

Sections don't have to be regularly sewn along a concertina, nor do they need to be a uniform size. The illustrated example utilizes the sculptural qualities of the folded book and experiments with the proportions between the folds and the sections. These folded books are pleasing and interesting to work with purely as forms, but they can also be used to emphasize artwork or a particular element or motif in your design.

venetian blind book

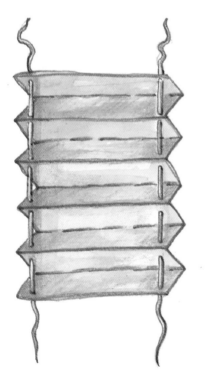

This style of binding is based on palm-leaf books made and used extensively in India and South-east Asia. Because of their fragility, not many early versions survive, so no one knows exactly how long they have been in use for making books. There are, however, beautiful lacquered examples from the eighteenth and nineteenth century in the British Library and other collections. The long, slim palm leaves were held together by threaded strings, much like a blind, except they were all single leaves. In the Venetian blind, the strings, ribbons, or sticks are threaded through a concertina fold.

single star book

The star book, so called for obvious reasons, has one fold of artwork per zigzag. You will need enough zigzag folds and pages to allow the book to form a complete circle. You could attach cover boards to this book, with ribbon ties to keep the book open in its star shape. See the Gallery Section on pages 80–81 for examples, or for a more complex version of the star book, see the 'Star Book' on page 118.

flag book

THIS BOOK IS FUN AND EASY TO make. It can be read like a conventional codex by turning over page by page but it also opens out into a panoramic sculptural form that is perfect for artwork and text. The flag book can become wonderfully architectural, if you turn it upside-down and open the flags in on one another.

MATERIALS

Greyboard

Covering paper for boards and board linings

Medium-weight paper for fold and strips

PVA glue

EQUIPMENT

Knife and/or scalpel

Steel safety ruler

Cutting mat

Dividers

Bone folder

Glue brushes

Pressing boards and a weight

1

Cut two boards to the required size and cover them with your chosen paper. Allow 1.5 cm (⅝ in) for the turn-ins and follow the instructions as for 'Pocket Fold Book' on page 27.

2

Cut your paper for the concertina fold to the required length (each side of the fold should be at least 2 cm (¾ in) wide) and 5 mm (³⁄₁₆ in) shorter than the board height. Fold the cut paper into a zigzag.

3

Glue the ends of the zigzag folds to the inside of the covered boards.

4

Cut a piece of paper for the strips 5 mm (³⁄₁₆ in) shorter than the height of the zigzag fold (this allows for a small gap between the flags to avoid them catching on each other when opening the book), and 5 mm (³⁄₁₆ in) narrower than the width of the boards. You will need one strip of paper for each of the folds in your zigzag book.

Decide how many flag strips you want on each of the folds and divide each page up equally.

4 5 6

Following the diagram below, glue the flags in position on to each of the folds. (A) and (B) strips are glued alternately on either side of the folds. Make sure you only glue about 1 cm (⅜ in) on the edge of each fold to avoid any glue showing when the pages are turned conventionally.

Cut two pieces of lining paper to fit inside the boards, making sure the end of the zigzag is covered. Glue in position and leave to dry between pressing boards under a weight.

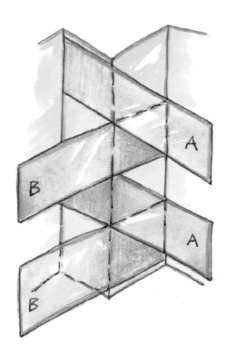

pop-up books

THIS BOOK IS BASED ON A SIMPLE FOLD and the three-hole pamphlet stitch. It contains small hidden panels which pop out when the pages are opened. The pages can be turned in sequence, or the book can stand up alone, with all the interiors on display. It could tell a story, contain a poem or display photographs instead of the paper panels.

MATERIALS

Heavy paper or thin card

Heavy paper or photographs for the panels

Sewing thread

Artwork

PVA glue

EQUIPMENT

Knife and/or scalpel

Steel safety ruler

Set square

Cutting mat or board

Sewing needle

Glue brush

1

Cut four pieces of card or paper 10 x 25 cm (4 x 10 in) and fold them each as illustrated.

(A) = 7.5 cm (3 in)

(B) = 5.3 cm (2⅛ in)

(C) = 1 cm (⅜ in)

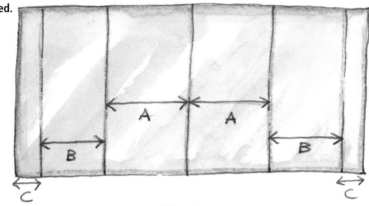

2

Cut windows, one in each of the four pages (here the window size is 3.5 x 6 cm (1⅜ x 2⅜ in). Then glue artwork, images or text on the panels adjacent to the windows.

Fold two pages inside each other as pictured, then fold the two remaining pages in the same way.

Make a paper sewing pattern for three-hole sewing to fit the centre fold of the pages. Make sewing holes in both sets, then sew all four pages together.

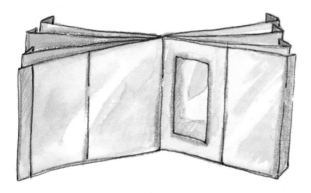

5

Cut four card inserts and attach image or text. If you are using the specified measurements, they should be 5.3 x 9.5 cm (2⅛ x 3¾ in). Turn the folds on the outer edges of the book in and apply glue to the insides (A). Then attach the card inserts to this glued edge.

Finally, glue the outer edge of (A) to the opposite flap and leave to dry thoroughly. To activate the pop-up, push the glued flaps towards the center of the book – the fold lines in the middle of each page will move outwards to form a triangle.

From left to right:

Sue Whittington and Margaret Benson's books are based on the star book format. The book in the foreground is designed using a series of cut-outs and a case binding. The second book has fold-out pages and is sewn on to boards covered in marbled paper.

Clare Bryan's 'Alice in Wonderland' is a dos-à-dos book made from an extended case binding.

Sue Doggett's books with uneven folds and additional sections sewn in, can extend the concertina fold in as many directions as you want.
Sue Doggett's 'Inamorato' is a bookwork made from the star

book format using photocopied acetates, collage, copper wire, hand-made paper pulp and dried lilies.

Helen Hutchins and Penny Stanford's 'Accordion Books' show how wooden pages offer an alternative tactile experience (left) and by printing on both sides of the concertina fold the text and image can work as a continuous story line (right).

containers

BOXES AND PORTFOLIOS ARE IDEAL for storing papers and objects, or protecting precious books. Even when storing serious contents, boxes needn't be dull and boring.

They can be both beautiful and hard-wearing, **perfect for anything** from account books to gift boxes.

If the container is for important documents, choose more durable materials, such as bookbinding cloth. Cloth comes in a variety of colours that can be embellished using decorative papers, ties and ribbons. For a sharp, stylish finish, try using eyelet fastenings or toggles. The two projects described in this chapter are a simple portfolio and a slipcase. This introduction teaches some basic techniques and there is a Japanese-style wrap-around case for you to experiment with later.

portfolio

THIS PORTFOLIO IS MADE FROM TWO BOARDS hinged with a cloth spine and covered with decorative paper. Inside are three flaps made from thick paper, which are creased and folded around your documents, notes or artwork to keep them safe and clean. The width of the spine will determine the storage capacity of the folio and the flaps can be folded to match.

MATERIALS

Cover board
Bookcloth for the spine
Thick paper for flaps
Paper for lining and covering boards
Ribbon or tape for ties
PVA glue
Wheatflour paste

EQUIPMENT

Knife and/or scalpel
Dividers
Bone folder
Pencil
Steel safety ruler
Chisel and hammer
Cutting mat
Pressing boards

1

Cut two boards to your chosen size, ours is 22.5 x 30 cm (9 x 12 in) with the grain direction running from head to tail.

2

To make the cloth spine piece, first decide how deep you want the portfolio to be (A). To this measurement add 10 cm (4 in) (B). This should be the width of the cloth. The length will be the height of the boards plus 4 cm (1½ in) (C). Cut the cloth to size.

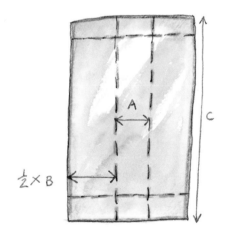

3

Set the dividers to 5 cm (2 in) and score lengthways along the edge of both boards (A). Apply glue to this area and lay the cloth down, lining it up with the scored line. Rub down well and then repeat on the other board.

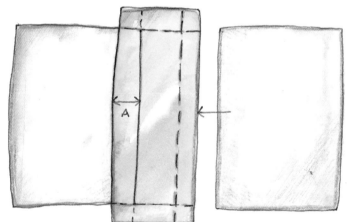

4

Trim the turn-ins to 1.5 cm (⅝ in), coat with glue and turn them over the board edges. Rub down.

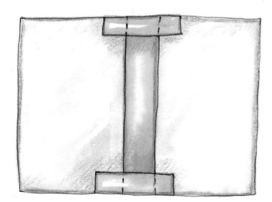

5

Cut another piece of bookcloth for the spine lining. This should be the same height as the boards and the width of the original spine piece. Coat the cloth with glue and stick it to the inside of the spine. Make sure you work the cloth into the board edges and rub down well across the spine.

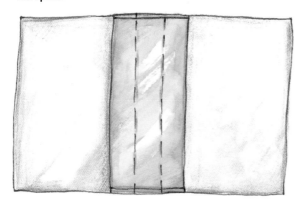

6

Cut two pieces of cover paper to overlap the spine cloth by 2 cm (⅛ in) (A) and to extend 2 cm (¾ in) past the board on the other three edges (B).

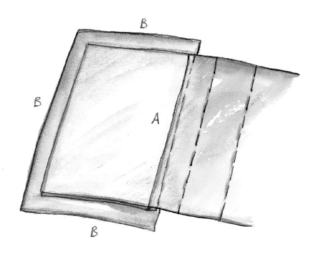

7

To avoid getting any glue on the cloth, coat the board with glue as far as the cloth edge, then run a little glue along the inside edge of the cover paper. Place the paper on the glued board, overlapping the cloth by 3 mm (⅛ in) and rub down well.

8

Trim the turn-ins to 1.5 cm (⅝ in) using a scalpel and safety ruler and fold, crease and cut the corners as illustrated.

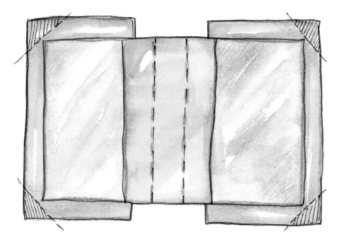

9

Now glue the turn-ins as before and leave the portfolio to dry under a weight between waxed or clean paper and pressing boards.

10

Cut two lengths of ribbon or tape for the ties, approximately 10 cm (4 in) long each. Find the centre of the board height and make a pencil mark 2 cm (¾ in) in from the board edge at this point. Using a knife or a hammer and chisel, make a slit over this point wide enough for the ribbon. Repeat on the other board so that the two slits are exactly opposite each other.

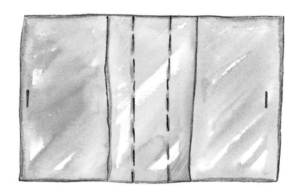

11

Pull the ribbons through the board (A), secure with glue and hammer flat (B).

12

For the flaps, cut three pieces of heavy paper the same width as the spine allowance (between the boards) (B), adding 2 cm (¾ in) for turn-ins (A) and 2.6 to 8.1 cm (2¼ to 3¼ in) for the folds (C) depending on the size of the portfolio. One of the pieces should be cut to the height of the board and the other two should be equal to the width. Score the above measurements on to the paper and crease. Mitre the inner corners of the turn-ins (see (D) below). Trim the flap edges as shown at (E) and make a zigzag by folding section (F) in half.

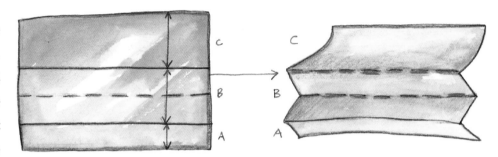

14

Cut two pieces of lining paper (with the grain direction running head to tail) to fit inside the boards. Measure the inside edges of the boards and cut the lining paper about 3 mm (⅛ in) narrower all around.

Paste the paper in position and rub down. Leave to dry overnight in the usual way. If you have large pressing boards, it is better to open out the portfolio and let it dry completely flat. It is also a good idea to leave the flaps and ribbons folded out when drying to avoid any unwanted indentations in the portfolio.

13

Coat the turn-ins of each flap with glue and place them on the right-hand board, lining the creased edge up with the edge of the board. Rub down well.

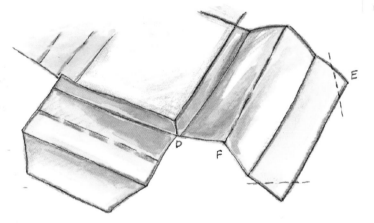

slipcase

A SLIPCASE FORMS A STRONG PROTECTIVE BOX for your books and it can be covered in paper or cloth. The boards are lined
before the box is assembled, which makes the construction simple. The most important thing here is accuracy
and, rather than calculating lots of small measurements, it is probably easier to use the dividers.

MATERIALS

Greyboard

Cover paper or
bookcloth

Lining paper

PVA glue

Masking tape

Medium-grit
sandpaper

EQUIPMENT

Knife and/or scalpel

Bone folder

Steel safety ruler

Dividers

Glue brush

Small stiff paintbrush

Drawing square

Pressing boards

Sanding block

1 Cover a piece of greyboard with your chosen lining
paper using glue. Rub it down well through clean paper
and leave it to dry between pressing boards under a
weight. To estimate the amount of paper needed,
measure twice the height of the book and add on 5 cm
(2 in) (A), and the width plus twice the thickness of the
book adding 5 to 5.6 cm (2 to 2¼ in) (B).

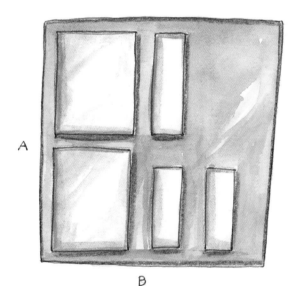

2 Measure the book for the slipcase from head to tail (A)
and from spine to fore edge (B). Also measure the
thickness (C).

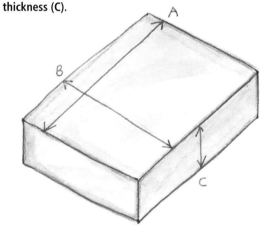

Cut the boards to size from the lined greyboard, following the measurements below. Make your measurements with the dividers.

1) Box sides (cut two)

(A) Height = height of book plus 2 board thicknesses plus 2 thicknesses of covering material

(B) Width = width of book plus 1 board thickness

2) Long wall (cut one)

(C) Height = same as height of box side

(D) Width = thickness of book plus 2 thicknesses of covering material

3) Short walls (cut two)

(E) Length = same as width of box side minus 1 board thickness

(F) Width = same as width of long wall

Cut or tear masking tape into lots of small pieces. Then, using a stiff paintbrush, apply glue to the edge of the long wall. Attach the long wall to one of the box sides and stick pieces of masking tape around the jointed boards.

Coat the edges of one of the short walls with glue, and attach it to the box side in the same way. Repeat with the remaining short wall.

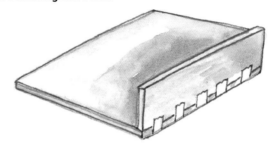

Coat the exposed edges of the walls already in place with glue and attach the second box side. When all the glue is dry, remove the masking tape carefully.

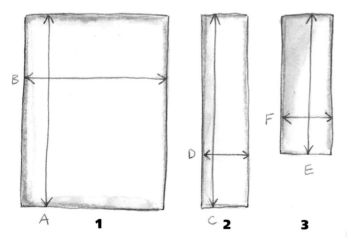

Any unevenness or rough edges will show through the paper or cloth so use medium-grit sandpaper and a sanding block to smooth the board edges before covering them.

Cut enough paper to cover the box as follows:

(A) = depth of box and (B) = 2 cm (¾ in).

Coat one side of the box with glue and apply your covering material leaving 2 cm (¾ in) for the turn-in. Rub down well before moving to the next stage. Then coat the spine of the box with glue and fold the covering material round, making sure you have no air bubbles at the joint. Rub down well. Finally, coat the second box side with glue and wrap the material round it, rubbing down as before.

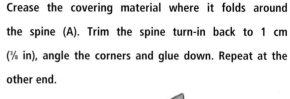

9

Crease the covering material where it folds around the spine (A). Trim the spine turn-in back to 1 cm (⅜ in), angle the corners and glue down. Repeat at the other end.

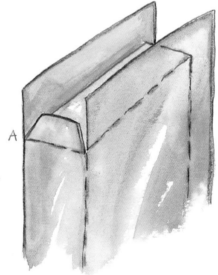

Cut one of the flaps of paper at the end of the box to fit the width of the short wall. Coat with glue and stick down, then trim the turn-in (A) back to the board edge at the open end of the box. Repeat at the other end.

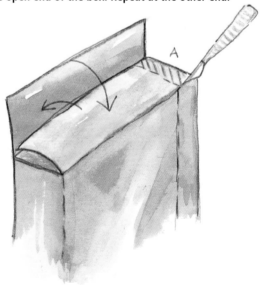

Cut the remaining two flaps of covering material to fit the width of the short wall, glue and rub down well. This time, do not trim at the open end of the box. Repeat at the other end.

Crease the material from the corners of the box (A) at the open end and cut along this line. Then measure one board thickness away from this cut on each side (B) and (C) and make a cut along that line. Repeat on all four corners.

Cut the small tabs in each corner to 6 mm (¼ in) and glue down as illustrated.

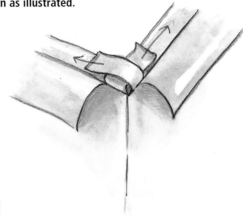

Coat the turn-ins with glue and fold them over the board edges, rubbing down well.

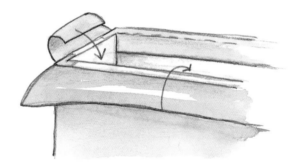

Leave the box to dry before slipping your book into it.

From left to right:

Clare Bryan's 'Open-closed Box' shows concertina folds enclosed in a CD case and then slotted into a slipcase made from printed greyboard.

Clare Bryan's 'Open-closed Books' are made from concertina fold books using cartridge paper and colour photocopies and brass eyelets.

Helen Hutchins' 'Three Books and Slipcase' are each case bound, single-section books with marbled paper covers in a slipcase.

Emma Ruffle's Japanese-style wrap-around case has carved wooden toggles and printed Japanese paper linings.

Sue Doggett's 'Mr Palomar Case' consists of three screen-printed books in a wooden case with compartmants and a sliding glass door.

the projects

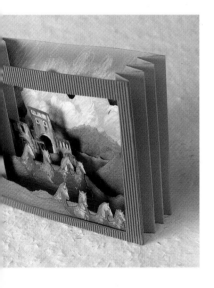

SO FAR YOU HAVE EXPERIENCED A NUMBER of different book structures and formats and some basic techniques for making them.

The next section consists of ten specific projects, described step-by-step,

which will utilize and develop these techniques.

Some new approaches have been added, including elements of design and new formats with which you can experiment. Although the projects are given titles, such as diary or journal, most of them are interchangeable. A sketchbook could be an album and an album could be a diary, for example. The size of each model is given at the beginning of each project, and the measurements in the instructions apply to a book of this size. Of course, you can change the scale, materials and sometimes even the sewing techniques to make your own version of each structure but it is probably a good idea to make a test piece first since the proportions will change.

All the projects in this section use greyboard that is approximately 5 mm ($\frac{3}{16}$ in) thick, except the 'Poem Book' and 'Rebinding a Book', which are made from a thinner 3 mm ($\frac{1}{8}$ in) board. Where techniques are repeated, you will be referred to the relevant section in the first half of the book or to the gallery sections for inspiration and other examples of a specified project. Create your own beautiful bookworks by drawing upon any of the techniques you have already experienced and all the new ideas you will want to experiment with from this section.

photograph album

an album is one of the most popular ways of
storing and displaying memorabilia such as
photographs, postcards, tickets
and so on but it can also be used as a visitors' book, journal or sketchbook.
The beauty of this structure is that it is expandable – you can add more pages when you need them.

The brass screw posts used to hold the binding together can be bought in various sizes so

that you can make your album exactly the thickness you want, and if you change your mind,

just add an extension post or two. The
model pictured is made using alternating
black and white pages and the boards are
covered in a three-colour paste paper. The
method for making paste papers is described
in the section on materials at the beginning
of the book. The spine boards are covered in
bookcloth which is extended to become a
strong, flexible hinge.

**The size of the model pictured is
23 x 17 x 2.5 cm (9⅛ x 6¾ x 1 in)**

1

Cut the paper for the pages to the required size adding on an extra 2 cm (¾ in) for the guards (A). Guards allow for the extra thickness of your mounted photographs or scraps, to stop the book from becoming wedge-shaped. Mark 2 cm (¾ in) in from the edge of the paper with the dividers. Using a steel ruler and bone folder, crease along the divider points and fold. Repeat for every page to form the guards.

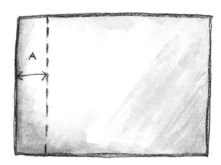

2

With the guards folded over, place pages inside each other as shown.

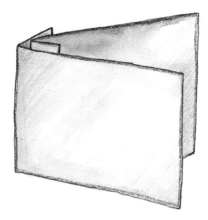

3

To determine the size of the brass posts, measure the total thickness of the folded pages (including the folded guards) and add roughly 6 mm (¼ in) to allow for the lined cover boards (A).

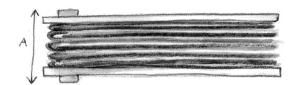

4

Cut two boards 3 mm (⅛ in) larger than the folded pages on all four sides. Measure 2.5 cm (1 in) in from the edge of each board and cut off (A); these are the spine boards. Then trim 5 mm (³⁄₁₆ in) off the width of the larger boards. This gives you the joint allowance (B).

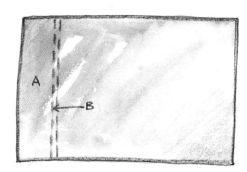

5

Measure the height of a spine board and divide into three (A). Then measure 12 mm (½ in) in from the long edge (B). These are the two points at which to drill holes for the brass posts.

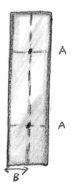

MATERIALS

Paper for pages, fairly heavy if you want to mount photographs

Greyboard

Decorative or coloured cover paper

Bookcloth for the spine and hinge

Paper for lining the boards inside

Brass posts and extensions

PVA glue

Wheatflour paste

Waxed paper

EQUIPMENT

Knife and/or scalpel

Steel safety ruler

Cutting mat or board

Dividers

Bone folder

Glue and paste brushes

G-clamps

Hand drill (or hole punch)

Pressing boards

6

Clamp the two spine boards together with the G-clamps over a pile of spare board. Put the spine board on which you marked the hole placement on top. Make two holes through the spine boards using a hand drill. If you use a hole punch, you will need to mark both boards and make the holes individually.

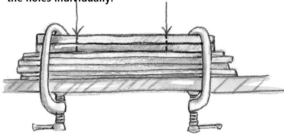

7

Stack your book sections, align them squarely at the folded edge and place on top of a pile of spare board. Cut a piece of greyboard the height of the folds and approximately 5 cm (2 in) wide (A). Lay this board on the folded edge of the book (B). Place one of the drilled spine boards over the book and greyboard, allowing for the 3 mm (⅛ in) square (C). Transfer the position of the holes from the spine board to the pages.

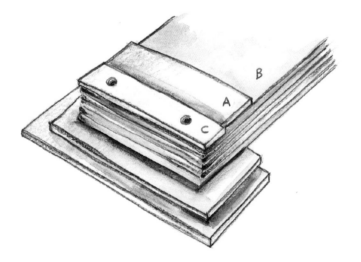

8

Remove the spine board and clamp the book and spare board in position at each end as before. Drill through. It is more difficult to use a hole punch for this job, but it can be done if you are accurate and careful. To do this, mark one section and punch out the holes. Then place it squarely on the next section and either mark where the holes are, or punch straight through. Continue, using the first section as a guide, until all sections are complete.

9

To cover the spine boards, cut two pieces of bookcloth larger than you need. Glue the boards to the cloth and trim the bookcloth to size, allowing 12 mm (½ in) turn-in (B) on three edges and 3 cm (1³⁄₁₆ in) on the other (A), which will form the hinge.

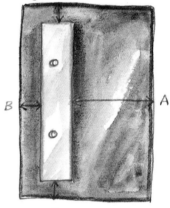

Cut the two corners at the spine edge, then turn over and glue as described in the 'Pocket Fold Book', on page 25.

11

Glue the back and front boards with your chosen cover paper, leaving a turn-in allowance of 1.5 cm (⅝ in). Cut the corners of one of the short edges on each board as shown in the diagram (A) and glue it down on to the board. Do not turn in the other edges yet.

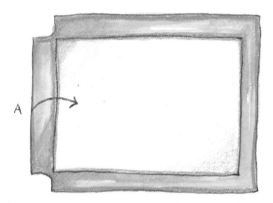

12

Glue the covered edge of the boards to the hinge cloth, leaving a 5 mm (³⁄₁₆ in) joint allowance (A). Trim the corners as before (B) and glue down the turn-ins. Leave to dry between waxed paper and pressing boards.

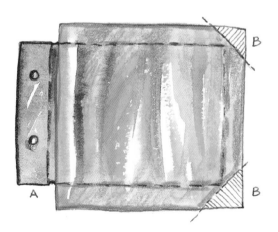

13

Cut two pieces of lining paper (with the grain direction running from head to tail) 3 mm (⅛ in) smaller than the cover boards on all four edges. Coat the papers with wheatflour paste and place in position. Rub down well, making sure the paper is worked into the joint. Leave to dry under a weight between waxed paper or blotting paper and pressing boards.

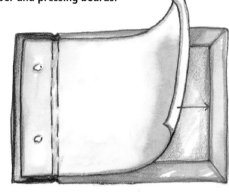

14

Punch or cut through the lining paper and bookcloth over the drilled holes and place the pages between the cover boards and insert the brass posts.

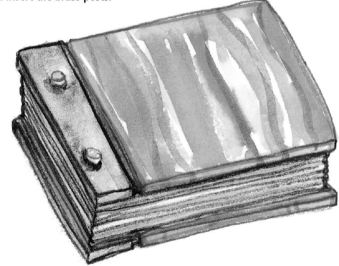

journal

this simple binding is ideal for daily or
occasional writing and personal notes
but, as with many of the other structures described here,
it can be used as a sketchbook or album just as effectively.

The cutout panel in the front board allows you to create a combined cover design and title page. The small image used on the front of this model is a lino cut made using water-based printing ink and hand-painted with watercolours. The image is mounted on a piece of Mexican bark paper that forms a visual link between the colour of the pages and the cover paper. The binding is elegant and easy to make using eyelets and a silk cord. Like the photograph album, this book can also be extended because there is no adhesive on the spine.

The size of the journal pictured here is 26 x 17.8 cm (7 x 10¼ in).

1

Cut and fold paper for the pages to size. This model has four sections of four pages, but you can use more. With dividers, mark in 2 cm (¾ in) from the folded edge of each section and, using a bone folder and ruler, score and crease along these points (A).

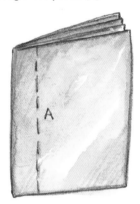

2

Measure the height of the book and divide into three. Punch or drill holes at the two points (A and B) through each section.

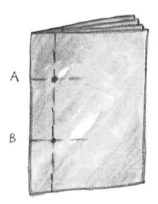

3

Cut two cover boards 3 mm (⅛ in) larger than the book all round. Using one section as a pattern, transfer the position of the holes to both boards and punch them out.

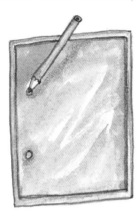

4

Measure 2 cm (¾ in) in from the spine edge of the board (where you have just punched the holes) and cut this strip away (A). Repeat with the other board, then put the spine strips to one side.

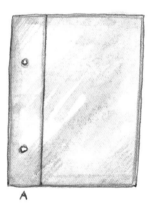

5

Trim away 5 mm (³⁄₁₆ in) from the edge of the two larger pieces of board (A) to produce the joint allowance.

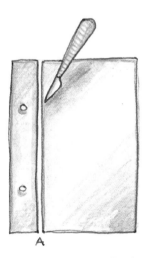

MATERIALS

Greyboard

Cover paper

Eyelets

Paper for pages

Lining paper

Waxed paper for pressing

Cord for binding

Print, drawing, photograph etc., for front cover

Masking tape

PVA glue and wheatflour paste

EQUIPMENT

Knife and/or scalpel

Cutting mat or board

Steel safety ruler

Bone folder

Dividers

Glue and paste brushes

Eyelet punch

Pressing boards

6

Mount your image on a piece of decorative paper and trim to size (here it is 4.5 x 5 cm (1¾ x 2 in).

7

To cut the window in the front board, find the centre point by dividing the board in half lengthways and widthways (A and B). Measure 1 cm (⅜ in) up from the centre line (C), position your artwork and add 5 mm (³/₁₆ in) to each edge. Cut out the area inside this border.

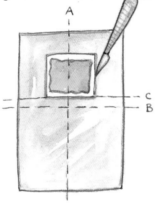

8

Cut two strips of bookcloth, 3 cm (1¼ in) wide and the height of the boards and attach one edge of each strip to each of the spine strips with glue.

9

Mark two points on the cloth 5 mm (³/₁₆ in) away from the edge of the spine piece (A). Coat the inside edge of the cover board with glue and attach to the cloth (B).

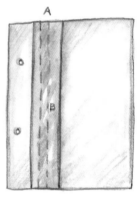

10

Cut four tiny strips of cover paper 3 x 8 mm (⅛ x ⁵/₁₆ in) and glue them around the inner corners of the window on the front board.

11

Cut two pieces of cover paper approximately 2 cm (¾ in) larger than the boards on all four sides. Coat the boards with glue and apply the paper, rubbing down well into the joints through a piece of clean paper. Trim the turn-ins to 1.5 cm (⅝ in), fold and cut the corners as usual and glue down the turn-ins. Leave the boards to dry under a weight between clean or waxed paper and pressing boards.

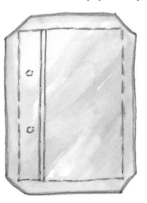

12

To turn in the cover paper at the window, trim the paper as illustrated, cutting diagonally into each corner. Trim the turn-ins to 1.5 cm (⅝ in) and glue down. Using a bone folder, carefully work the paper into the corners of the window. When the glue is dry, trim the turn-ins on the inside of the boards back to 3 mm (⅛ in) for neatness.

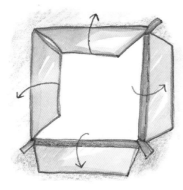

13

Cut two pieces of lining paper 3 mm (⅛ in) smaller than the boards on all four edges. Place one of the linings in position on the front board and anchor it temporarily with masking tape. Turn the board over and transfer the size of the cutout to the lining paper by scoring around the edge of the window with a bone folder. Remove the paper from the board and peel off the masking tape.

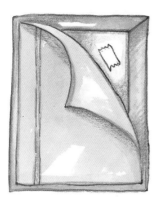

14

Cut out the square from the lining paper, taking away an extra 1 mm (¹⁄₁₆ in) to allow for the thickness of the cover paper. Coat the lining papers with wheatflour paste, position them on the boards and rub down. Press, then leave under a weight between waxed or blotting paper and pressing boards to dry.

15

Cut through the paper covering the punched holes and work the excess into the recesses, then press in the eyelets using an eyelet punch.

16

Paste your artwork into position on the front page of your book and leave to dry under a weight between waxed paper and pressing boards.

17

To finish your journal, take the cord through the eyelets as illustrated in the diagram, knotting both ends to prevent them from fraying.

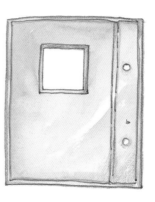

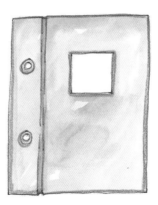

scrapbook

this binding was made using a variety of hand-made papers with just a hint of colour to **bring out the warmth of the natural materials.** The ties are made from hemp cord knotted and embellished with a broken necklace from Thailand and a few wooden beads and the clasp is made from a piece of driftwood found on a beach in Wales.

A scrapbook can contain papers of considerable thickness, as long as it has corresponding guards at the spine to accommodate the extra bulk, and stop the book becoming wedge-shaped. The guards in this model are made from Indian silk paper and scraps of the cover paper. The guards are torn instead of cut, which gives them a softer appearance more in keeping with the feel of the book.

The size of the scrapbook pictured here is 24 x 17 x 1 cm (9½ x 6¾ x ⅜ in).

1

Fold the paper for the pages. Tear the guards to size and place a guard (or two if the papers are very thin) between each fold of paper. Assemble into sections.

2

Sew the sections to cords or thongs following steps 1 to 3 of 'Sewing over Cords or Thongs', using matching sewing thread.

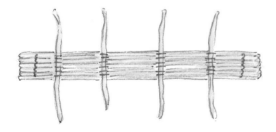

3

Cut two boards 3 mm (⅛ in) larger than the pages at the head, foot and fore edge. Mark the boards for lacing in the cords and cut recesses on the front and back of the board as described in steps 1 to 4 of 'Cutting Recesses'. Cover the boards, cutting and gluing corners and turn-ins as described in steps 4 to 8 of the 'Pocket Fold Book'.

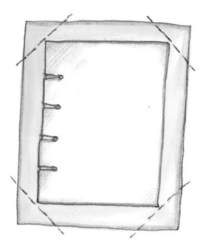

4

Lace on your covered boards as described in steps 2 to 5 of 'Lacing-in Boards'.

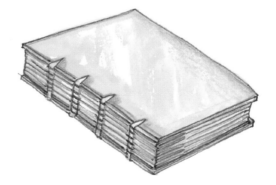

5

Make the clasp by drilling two holes through the driftwood or dowelling with a small drill. You will need to clamp the wood down to hold it in position and remember to use plenty of spare boards to protect your work surface.

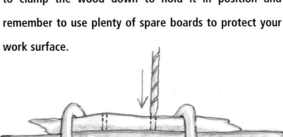

6

Make two ties, five times the width of the book, from twine, cord, threads or string and tie one at each end of the clasp (A). Then take the two ties to the back cover board and mark sewing positions (B).

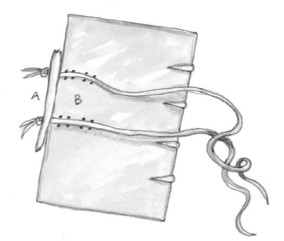

7

Drill or use a bodkin to make the sewing holes through the cover board.

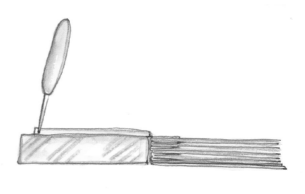

8

Attach the ties with stitching of your choice, using coloured thread. You may need to sew through, as well as over, the ties since they may slide around.

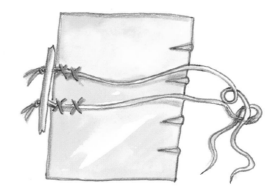

Wrap the ties around the book, knotting and beading the cords as you go. When you are happy with how the ties look, unwrap them.

10

The next step is filling-in, which is optional and can be applied to many projects in this book. Filling-in gives a stylish finish to the insides of the boards and allows you to remove lumps and bumps caused by lacing-in and sewing. To make fillers, see 'Attaching Boards' and follow steps 1 to 3 of 'Fill-ins'.

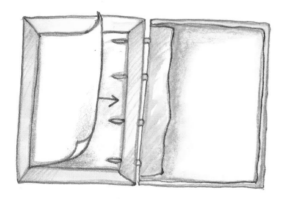

Cut the endpapers the same size as the pages of the book. Paste them down with wheatflour paste and put a sheet of waxed or blotting paper between them. Then put a piece of thick, protective paper (with a torn edge) under the ties on the back board to avoid any unwanted impressions. Put the book under a weight between waxed paper and pressing boards to dry overnight. When the endpapers are dry, the book can be tied and the cords wrapped around the wooden clasp.

four books in a box

japanese sewing techniques are among the most decorative to work,
and you have already seen the four-hole pattern
on page 53. Here, the project has been extended to include three
other methods of sewing and a wrap-around box.

The papers used in the models are a mixture of Japanese and hand-made Indian varieties
and they are sewn together with contrasting embroidery thread. To tear the paper in a

straight line, wet it first with a damp
paintbrush against a ruler to release the
fibres and give you a mock deckle edge. The
collage design is applied with wheatflour
paste. The sewing patterns need to be
accurate to look good, so you must be
careful when placing the holes. Using the
same proportions for each of the books and
scoring the base line of each pattern with a
bone folder will help you achieve a perfect
finish. The wrap-around box is simple to
make and can be covered in cloth or paper
and fastened with ribbon, toggles or twisted
threads. In this example, an element of the
book design is repeated on the cover.

**The books pictured are 9.5 x 19 x 0.3 cm
(3¾ x 7½ x ⅛ in).**

1

Make the pages and cover as described in 'Japanese-style Sewing' on page 53. If you are going to add artwork or include torn and folded pages, do this before any sewing so the paste can dry thoroughly. Leave pasted papers to dry between sheets of blotting paper under weighted pressing boards.

2

Follow steps 2 to 6 of 'Japanese-style Sewing' to complete the sewing pattern for Yotsume Toji (four-hole binding).

3

Make sewing holes in the other three books as illustrated. (A) is called Kangxi Toji (noble binding), (B) is Asa-no-ha Toji (hemp-leaf binding) and (C) is called Kikko Toji (tortoiseshell binding).

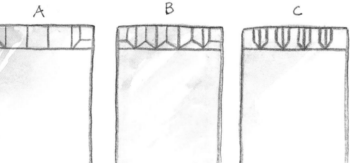

4

To sew the Kangxi Toji pattern, work as the Yotsume Toji to the corners, then take threads through the extra sewing hole as illustrated.

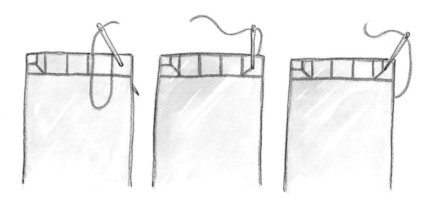

MATERIALS

Paper for pages and cover

Embroidery thread

Greyboard

Cloth or paper for box covering

Heavy paper for box side wraps

PVA glue

Wheatflour paste for collage (optional)

Threads, ribbon etc., for ties

Blotting paper

Waxed paper

EQUIPMENT

Knife and/or scalpel

Cutting mat or board

Steel safety ruler

Bone folder

Dividers

Sewing needle

Glue brush

Hammer

Pressing boards and a weight

5

To work the sewing patterns of Asa-no-ha Toji, follow the instructions for Kangxi Toji and then proceed as shown in the diagrams. Finish off in the usual way.

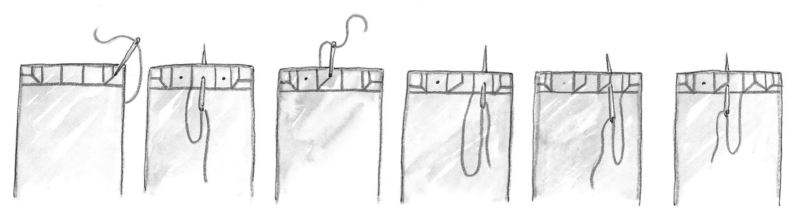

6

The pattern for Kikko Toji is worked in figures of three stitches as illustrated. Finish off as before.

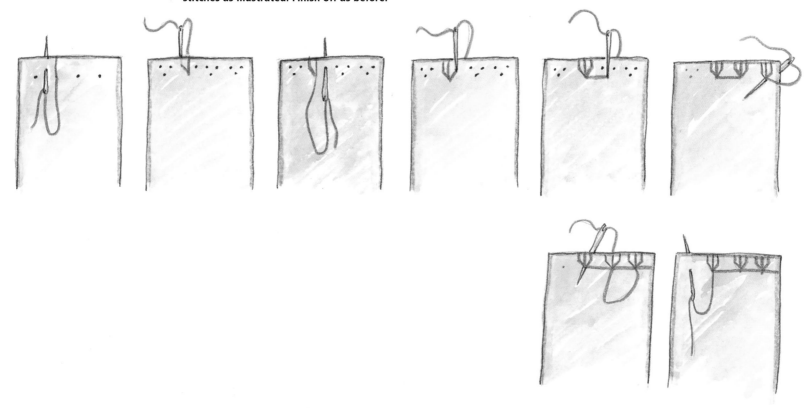

Place the books on top of one another and measure head to tail, spine to fore edge and their combined thickness. The sizes of the boards for the box should be as follows (all boards are the same height):

(A) Inner lid   = Spine to fore edge of the books

(B) Base   = (A) plus one board thickness

(C) Outer lid   = (A) plus two board thicknesses

(D) Spine wall   = Combined thickness of all four books

(E) Fore edge wall = (D) plus one board thickness

(F) Height   = Height of the books plus two board thicknesses

Cut the boards with the grain direction running from head to tail.

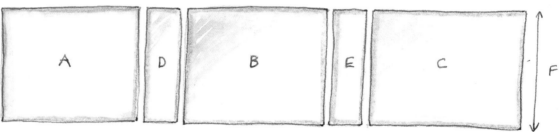

Cut the covering material slightly larger all round than the boards and glue each board down on it as shown, leaving a 3 mm (⅛ in) gap between each piece. Rub down well. Trim the turn-ins to 2 cm (¾ in), cut the corners as usual and glue down each of the four sides. Leave to dry under a weight between waxed paper and pressing boards.

9

Cut two pieces of heavy paper for the top and bottom wraps that hold the books in place. These should be slightly narrower than the width of the box base (A) and the same height (B), plus the combined thickness of the books (C) and a 2 cm (¾ in) turn-in allowance (D). Using a bone folder and ruler, crease along these lines.

10

Coat the turn-in allowance with glue and attach to the head and tail of the box base. The wraps can be shaped if you prefer.

11

On the outside, make slits or holes (depending on your method of fastening) 1 cm (⅜ in) in from the edge of the outer board, either one in the centre or two – one at the head and tail (A). Then make corresponding slits or holes in the centre of the spine wall (B). Thread the ties through and glue to the inside of the boards. Hammer flat.

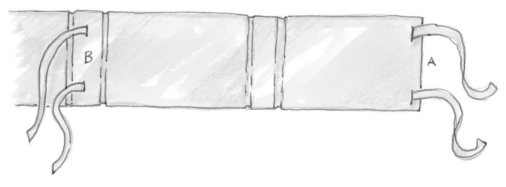

12

Cut two pieces of covering material to line the spine and fore edge walls. The length is 6 mm (¼ in) shorter than the height of the box and the width is that of the spine or fore edge wall plus 3.5 cm (1⅜ in). The corners can be cut to a 45-degree angle if desired. Glue and position over the two walls, rubbing down well into the joints.

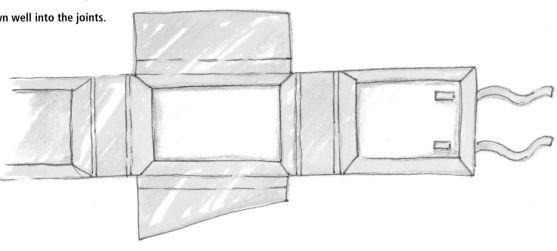

13

Cut three pieces of lining paper to cover the inside of the boards, 3 mm (⅛ in) smaller than the boards on all four sides. Fold the top and bottom wraps to the front so that they do not get glue on them. Coat the linings with paste or glue and attach them to the boards. Rub down well through clean paper and leave to dry under a weight between waxed or blotting paper and pressing boards.

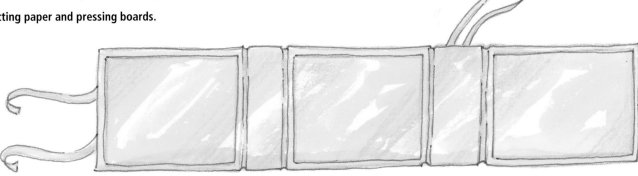

theatre book

this book form is reminiscent of a toy theatre
and is also called a tunnel book because of its telescopic nature.
There are many applications for this unusual format.
It can be closed to form a three-dimensional picture or opened out
to become a theatre set for your own production.

The artwork in this model is a collage made from a variety of materials – torn paper,

watercolour pencils and altered photocopies – and is based loosely on a holiday in Italy. You

could use family photographs to make an

unusual portrait or reduce the scale to form

a fantasy greetings card or story book. The

structure is based around two concertina

folds that support a series of panels.

**The theatre book pictured here is
26 x 21 x 21 cm (10¼ x 8¼ x 8¼ in) fully extended.**

1 Decide on your imagery or design and gather together all the collage materials you need. Make the panels, starting with the back one (shown here as sky) which is full size. Add an extra 2 cm (¾ in) to the width of each panel, except the back one (A) to form tabs. These form a hinge which will attach the artwork to the side concertina folds of the book. The pictured model has five panels including the back one; it is probably best to limit the number during your initial experimentation so that the image doesn't become too complicated. Before cutting, glue all your artwork to thin card and leave between pressing boards to dry.

MATERIALS

Greyboard

Thin card for mounting artwork

Photographs, artwork, collage materials etc., for the panels

Heavy paper for the concertina folds

PVA glue

Paint, coloured pencils etc., if desired

EQUIPMENT

Knife and/or scalpel

Steel safety ruler

Cutting mat or board

Dividers

Bone folder

Glue brushes

Paintbrushes (optional)

Pressing boards

2 Working forward from the back to the front, cut each panel smaller as you work towards the front of the book. Since the panels are of different heights, you will need to cut your tabs accordingly. If you wish, you can round off the top edge of the tab for a neat finish (A). Fold back along the edge of each panel.

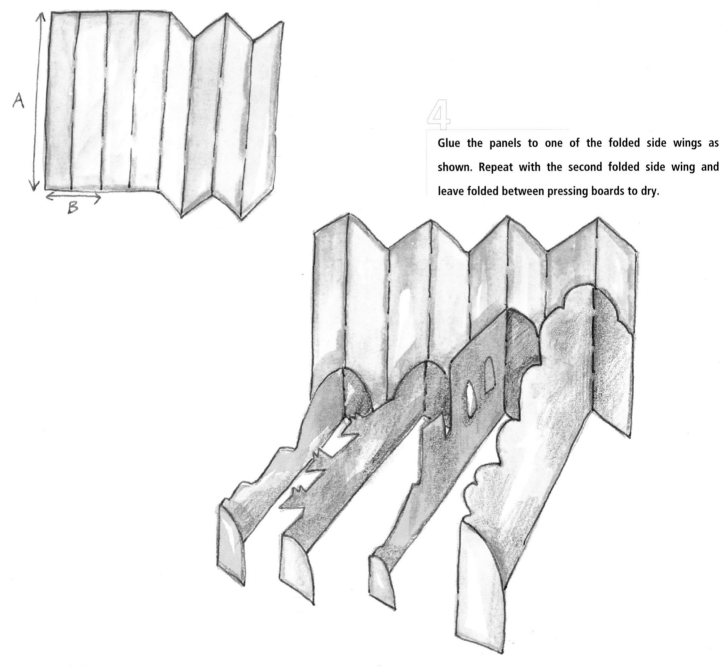

3

Fold two concertinas for the side wings, the same height as the back panel (A). In the model, each fold measures 5 cm (2 in) (B). If you are making a smaller book, reduce the width a little to give it visual balance. You will need one fold for each panel, not including the back one.

4

Glue the panels to one of the folded side wings as shown. Repeat with the second folded side wing and leave folded between pressing boards to dry.

5

Apply glue to the half-fold of each concertina panel at the back (A) and attach them to the last panel that forms the backdrop (B).

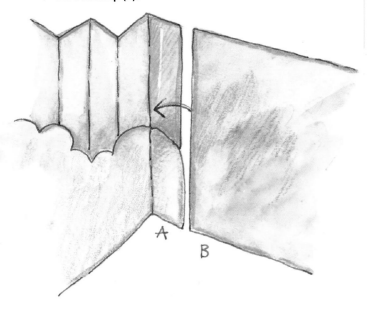

7

If your front board has sides which are narrower than the fold you will need to trim the concertina folds to fit (A). Glue the trimmed half-folds and attach the front board, rubbing down well. Leave between waxed paper and boards to dry.

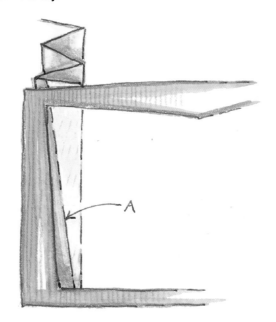

6

To finish the front of the book, cut a piece of greyboard the same size as the back panel (A). Cut out a central area, which allows you to see all your artwork (B). The board in the model is covered with corrugated paper to give the impression of curtains. This paper is cut flush with the edge of the board, which has been painted a contrasting colour.

Here the inside of the board has been shaped slightly. You can cut yours to whatever design suits the theme of your book. It can even be a continuation of the image.

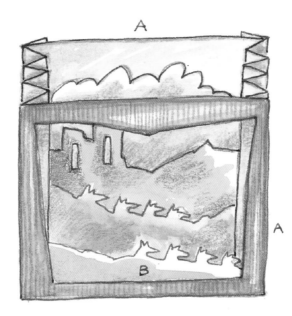

star book

this version of the star book is based on a triple concertina fold and is a fun format for cards, story books or poems. **It can be read coventionally by turning over one page at a time or displayed in its sculptural form, which makes it ideal for artwork**.

The example here is an imaginary planetary landscape with shooting stars made from foam rubber. The main composition of the book is made using a collage of hand-made paper, photocopies, copper wire and watercolours. Each fold is a different width, so the images become three-dimensional, with the smallest at the front and the largest at the back. They are held in place by a pamphlet stitch at the front fold and are protected by two covered boards. Have a look in the gallery sections for other interpretations of this format and then let your own imagination run wild. The possibilities for fantastic landscapes and interiors are limitless.

The size of the book shown here is 11 x 13 x 3 cm (4³⁄₈ x 5¹⁄₈ x 1¹⁄₈ in) when closed and approximately 85 cm (33¹⁄₂ in) long when fully extended.

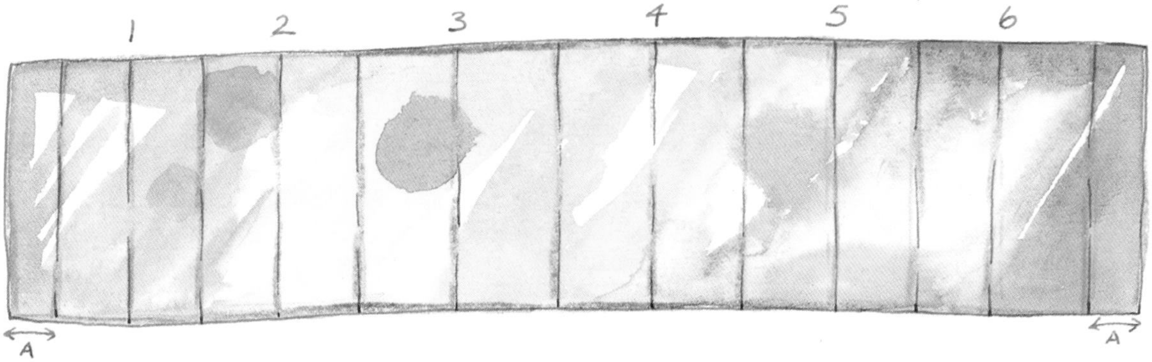

1

Design and make three panels. Start with the background. Decide on the number of folds you want. Here it is six, with the width of each page (half a fold) measuring 10.3 cm (4⅛ in). Allow an extra 2.5 cm (1 in) at each end of your length of paper, which will be attached to the boards (A). You could have cutouts in this back fold but it must remain strong enough to support the other, more fragile folds. Fold into a concertina as described in the chapter on folding.

2

Next, design and make the other two panels which relate visually to the background wall. You need the same number of folds as before, but this time they are gradated in size. The width of each page on the front fold is 7 cm (2¾ in), whilst the pages of the central fold are 8.5 cm (3⅜ in) in width. Fold the concertina folds to size, keeping in mind that the difference in size between the back (A) and middle (B) folds should be greater than between the middle and front (C) folds. Before the pictured model was sewn together, the edges of each fold were painted with acrylic paint to emphasize the star shape and hide all traces of the white paper.

3

Make a sewing pattern as described in 'Pamphlet Sewing', using the height of the fold to calculate the sewing points. Put all three folds of paper together and, using a needle, make the holes for sewing.

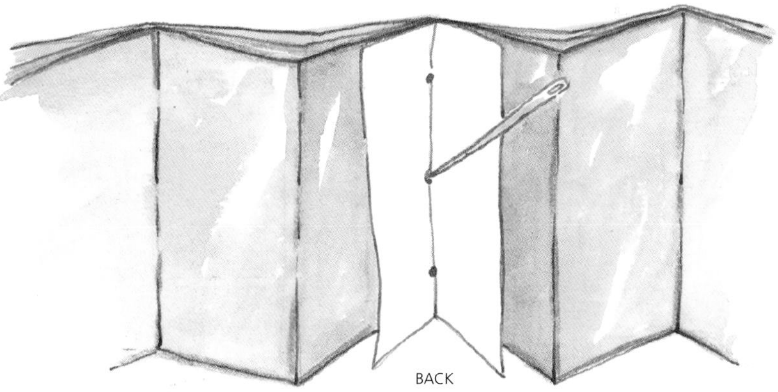

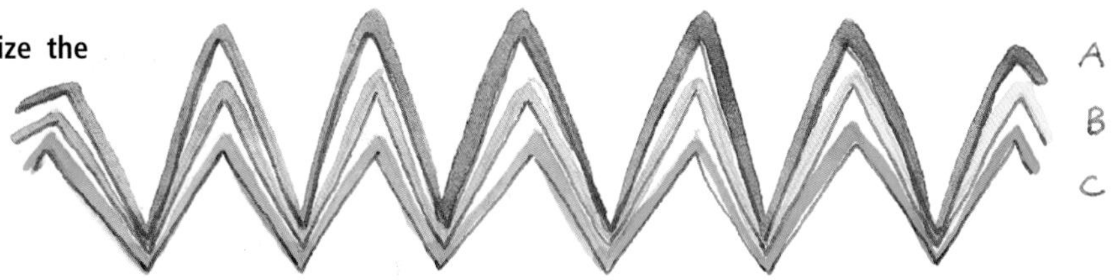

MATERIALS

Materials for collage and artwork

Heavy paper for the folds

Coloured thread (waxed)

Greyboard

Thin card

Cover paper or bookcloth

Waxed paper

PVA glue

EQUIPMENT

Knife and/or scalpel

Dividers

Cutting mat or board

Bone folder

Glue brush

Sewing needle

4

Sew the book together. The knots can be hidden or used as part of the design so you can choose to have them at the front or the back.

6

Cut two boards 1 mm ($\frac{1}{16}$ in) larger than the book on all four sides and cover with paper or cloth, turning in only one of the long edges (A).

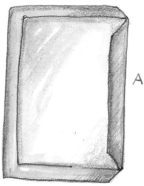

5

Glue each of the 2.5 cm (1 in) folds together (A), rubbing them down well.

7

Measure the thickness of the small folds with the dividers and find a piece of thin card to match and act as a filler.

8

Apply glue to the back of the small folds and attach them to the covered edge of the boards, inside the 1 mm (¹⁄₁₆ in) allowance made in step 6.

9

Cut two pieces of filler card to fit the area between the board edges and the small fold at both ends. Glue in position and leave under a weight to dry.

10

Trim the remaining turn-ins to 1.5 cm (⅝ in), cut the corners and glue them down.

11

Cut two pieces of lining paper to fit the inside of the boards. Paste down and leave to dry under weighted boards between sheets of waxed or blotting paper.

diary with a clasp

a clasp inspired by medieval jewellery and richly painted endpapers
will turn a standard case-binding
into a personal, gothic-style book of hours
that you will enjoy writing in every day.

The clasp itself is made from twisted copper wire and upholstery nails (with most of the pin cut off) on a base of thin card and the strap is made from two layers of bookcloth painted the same colours as the clasp. The back of the clasp and strap are then lined with felt and attached to the board with glue and silk and thread. An extension to the design is embossed on the cover board using shaped scraps of greyboard. Of course, you can experiment with brass or silver wire, coloured glass or old pieces of jewellery; and the design of the clasp can be simple and elegant with just a few twists of wire or highly wrought like this one.

**The size of this diary is
17 x 15 x 1.5 cm (6¾ x 6 x ⅝ in).**

1

Fold, cut, press and sew the pages of the diary as described in 'Sewing on Tapes', on pages 48–49.

2

For the clasp cut two pieces of thin card to your desired shape and decide upon the width of the strap, (here 2 cm (¾ in)). Cut two pieces of cloth twice this width and approximately 10 cm (4 in) long, then glue them together. Fold both edges around to meet in the centre; crease and glue down. Press for a couple of minutes.

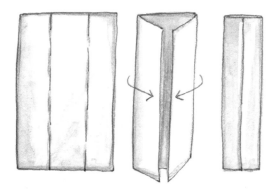

3

Glue the strap to one of the card shapes made in step 2 (A). Then cut another piece of thin card the same size as (A) but cut to fit around the end of the strap (B). Glue this down. Finally glue the second card shape over the top of (B) so the strap is sandwiched between (C).

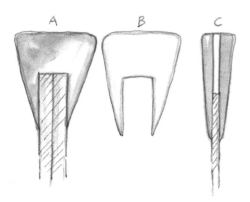

4

Cover the clasp with glued, crumpled paper and wind the wire around and through the shaped board, adding upholstery tacks or whatever you have chosen to use. Paint the clasp and strap with acrylics, then wipe it from the wire. Continue painting and wiping until you have achieved the effect you want.

5

Glue a piece of over-sized felt to the back of the clasp and strap and, when the glue is dry, trim the felt to size. Put to one side.

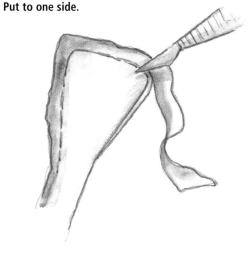

MATERIALS

Greyboard

Bookcloth

Paper for pages

Decorated endpapers

Linen sewing thread

Mull

Kraft paper

Thin card

Materials for clasp

Acrylic paints

Copper wire

Felt to match or contrast with the bookcloth

Waxed paper

PVA glue

Wheatflour paste

Matching Velcro

EQUIPMENT

Knife and/or scalpel

Steel safety ruler

Cutting mat or board

Bone folder

Dividers

Glue and paste brushes

Sewing needle

Wire cutters and pliers (optional)

A piece of thick foam, bigger than the size of the cover boards

Press or pressing boards and G-clamps

Hammer (and chisel, optional)

6

Make a pair of decorative endpapers using one of the techniques described in 'Paper' or use commercially printed papers and attach them to the book as described in 'Attaching Endpapers', page 58. To glue the spine, trim the book (if preferred), line the spine and cut the cover boards; follow steps 2 to 7 of the case binding project on pages 62–63.

7

Before gluing on the second board, you need to add the cutout shape which forms the raised area. Using the clasp as a pattern, extend the design on to a piece of thin card and cut it out. Glue this shape in position on the front board.

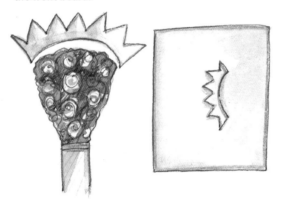

8

So that the strap sits securely and neatly on the back board, it is advisable to cut a recess in the board. To do this, mark the centre point of the long edge of the board (A) and position the strap so that the centre of it lines up with point (A). Add just under 3 mm (⅛ in) on each side of the strap and mark with a couple of divider points (B). The recess on the model is 4.5 cm (1¾ in) long but you can make it longer or slightly shorter, if you wish (C).

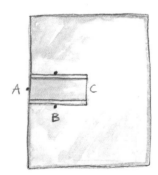

9

Measure the thickness of the strap with the dividers and cut the same thickness of board out of the recess. Using a strong knife, or a hammer and chisel, cut through at point (A) and cut the recess as marked in step 8.

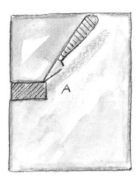

10

Turn the board over and make another recess the same width as before and 2.5 cm (1 in) long, towards the spine edge, away from the slit (A).

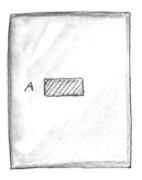

11

Cut your covering cloth 2 cm (¾ in) bigger all round than the area of the boards and spine. Use steps 8 to 12 in 'Case Binding' on pages 63–64, but this time, the cover boards need to be pressed as you glue them. If you don't have a press, use pressing boards and two G-clamps. When you have applied the cloth, place the cover board cloth side up on a pressing board (A), lay the foam over the top (B) and cover it with another pressing board (C). Place in the press or between two clamps and tighten until the foam is almost flat. Leave for 10 to 15 minutes. Do this on both front and back boards, attaching the spine piece in the centre, and leave it to dry under a weight between waxed paper and pressing boards.

12

Place the pages of the diary prepared in step 1 in the completed case and measure the required length of the strap. This will be from (A) to (B) to (C) in the diagram. Place the clasp in position, take the strap around the fore edge of the book and through the slit at (B). Cut the strap to fit into the inner recess, glue and hammer flat.

13

Glue the strap into the recess on the outside of the board. If you wish, you can add decorative stitches made from silk thread or painted twine, taking them through the board and recessing them on the inside of the board.

14

Trim the mull and the tapes to an equal length and put down the endpapers as in steps 14 to 16 of 'Case Binding' on page 65. Make sure you press the book with the strap undone using the foam or you won't get an even pressing.

15

The next day, when the book is thoroughly dry, glue a small piece of Velcro to the front board and the back of the clasp to act as a fastening. The book is now ready to use.

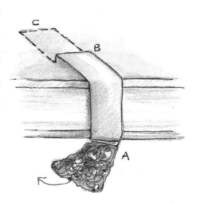

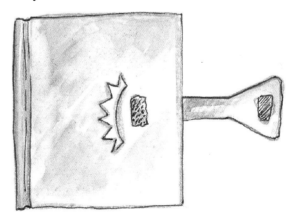

address book with notepad

make a large address book to keep beside the telephone
or a small portable version like the one pictured.
Either way, you will find it effective and easy to use,
having designed it to your own specifications.

The example here is covered with alphabet paper made from a photocopied collage overlaid with hand-made Japanese paper. This can be personalized with your or a friend's initials, drawings, maps or a simple repeat pattern. If you cover the book with paper and are going to use it every day, a slipcase (as described in the chapter on containers) would slow wear and tear to prolong its life; or you could use a bookcloth for extra strength and durability. There is the additional advantage of having a removable notepad with tear-off pages for quick notes and telephone messages, and when the pages run out, simply add more; you could also use the pocket for maps, guides, stamps or business cards. The tabs are unmarked in the model, but you can organize and label your index by collage, calligraphy or typed symbols to suit your needs.

The size of the example here is
13.5 x 11.5 x 2 cm (5⁵⁄₁₆ x 4½ x ¾ in).

1

Fold and cut paper for pages and make eight sections with three folds in each. Align and trim the fore edges. Then cut one fold for each section, using heavy paper, the same height and 1.5 cm (⅝ in) wider than the page size (A).

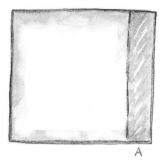

A

2

Cut the folds as shown to form the index and place in the centre of each section.

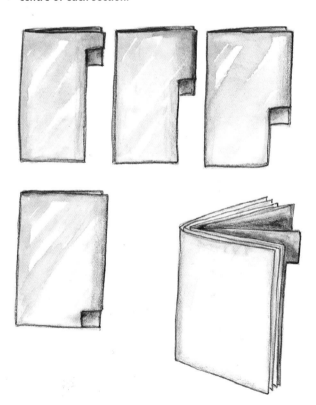

3

Sew the book on to tapes (three in this example) as described in 'Sewing on Tapes', page 48.

4

Make the notepad by cutting single sheets of paper roughly the same size as the book and gluing them together at one end.

5

Cut a piece of the heavy paper the same size as the notepad. Lay a sheet of waste paper 1 cm (⅜ in) away from the glued edge of the pad, brush the exposed edge with glue and attach the heavy paper. Press.

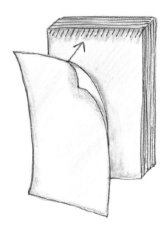

6

Cut a piece of the Japanese cover paper the same height as the notepad (A), adding on the spine thickness (B) and 18 mm (¾ in) (C). Glue it to the heavy paper backing. Trim the notepad 6 mm (¼ in) smaller than the book on the three unglued edges.

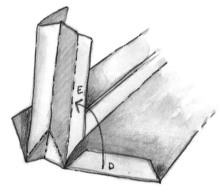

7

Make the pocket from cloth, heavy paper or lined plain paper and cut to size as shown in the diagram.

(A)	=	Half the height of the notepad
(B)	=	The width of the notepad plus 1 cm (⅜ in).
(C)	=	The thickness of the notepad plus 3 mm (⅛ in)
(D)	=	1 cm (⅜ in) turn-in
(E)	=	(A) (Proportions not exact on diagram)
(F)	=	2.5 cm (1 in) turn-in

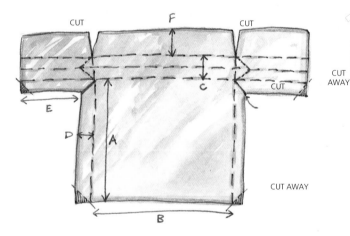

8

Score the lines with a bone folder, crease to form the pocket folds and turn-ins as shown then glue (D) to (E) and press.

9

Cut one endpaper for the back of the book as usual (A). The front endpaper needs an extra width of paper to accommodate the thickness of the notepad (B). Measure and cut accordingly. Attach the endpapers with glue.

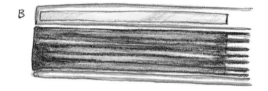

10

Trim the inner fold of each endpaper back to the width of the book to expose the index tabs (A).

Apply glue to the spine of the book, trim the head and tail if required and line the spine with mull and Kraft paper as described in the 'Case Binding' on page 62. Trim the mull and tapes to an equal width using a piece of board to protect your endpapers.

Make a collage using paper large enough to cover the book with approximately 2 cm (¾ in) extra for turn-ins. Photocopy it (or use another decorative paper that won't smudge when damp), apply wheatflour paste to it and lay the Japanese paper over it, rubbing down well. Place blotting paper on each side and press. Then leave to dry between pressing boards and under a weight, changing the blotting paper frequently until it is dry.

Cut two cover boards 6 mm (¼ in) longer than the height of the book and 3 mm (⅛ in) narrower than the width. Place the notepad and pocket on top of the book with a cover board on each side. Measure the combined thickness (A) for the width of the spine piece, which will be the same height as the cover boards. Make the case as described on page 64.

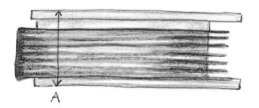

14

Paste and put down the back endpaper as usual, press and leave it weighted to dry. Lay the book on the back board and drop the front board back. Paste the endpaper then stand the book on its spine. Put the endpaper down with the board open as shown, supporting the book block with a weight. Make sure the endpaper is worked into the joint (A) and forms a right angle with the book without pulling. Cover with waxed or blotting paper, a pressing board and weight and leave to dry in the open position.

15

When the endpaper is completely dry, glue in the pocket. Once the glue dries, place the notepad in the pocket. The book is now ready to use.

poem book

the poem book is designed to reveal each page in sequence but it **can also be read, fully extended, in a different order.** The text in the poem book below comes from nineteenth-century book catalogues that were cut up to create a new story, and is sandwiched between two sheets of thin acetate that are machine sewn together.

Alternatively, you could attach the panels using wire, rivets or eyelets and thread various materials or wires through the holes. You can use collage, calligraphy, photocopies or a typewriter to produce your text (and/or images), which can be constructed like the example here or glued to panels of decorative or hand-made paper. Although the structure is called a poem book, it would work equally well with photographs, prints or drawings as a hanging book or frame. You can experiment with the shape of the windows; the format stays the same.

The size of this poem book is 9.5 x 7.5 x 2.8 cm (3¾ x 3 x 1⅛ in) when closed, and 29.5 x 30 x 0.1 cm (11¾ x 12 x ¹⁄₁₆ in) open.

1

Choose your poem or text. Arrange the text in panels and mount each one on decorative paper with glue or sew them between two layers of acetate. In the example, the threads are left uncut as part of the design, but they can be knotted and trimmed if you prefer.

2

Cut a piece of paper and mark with the same number of panels as your text. Set the text panels over the paper in the pattern you desire, vertically, horizontally, in a particular order or none at all. Use the paper to experiment with cuts and folds until you have the pattern you want. This example uses two T-shaped cuts as shown, to help fold the book up neatly.

3

Cut the greyboard into the required number of pieces for the panels, allowing for a frame of at least 1 to 1.5 cm (⅜ to ⅝ in) around each piece of text (A). The boards should all be the same size. Measure the largest piece of text and leave a small margin around it (B), then cut windows from each board to this measurement (C).

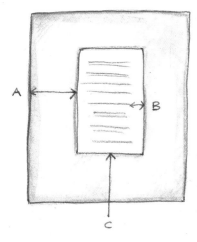

4

Cut small strips of the covering paper and cover the inner corners of the windows as described in step 10 of the 'Journal' project on page 102.

Cut small strips of the covering paper and cover the inner corners of the windows as described in step 10 of the 'Journal' project on page 102.

MATERIALS

Text and/or images

Thin acetate or decorative/hand-made paper

Thin greyboard

Cover paper

Lining paper

Coloured threads (for machine and hand sewing)

Waxed paper for pressing

PVA glue

EQUIPMENT

Knife and/or scalpel

Cutting mat or board

Bone folder

Dividers

Sewing needle

Sewing machine (optional)

Glue brush

Pressing boards

5

The example on page 130 is made from six pairs of jointed boards attached to each other by paper hinges. To make each pair, cut a piece of the cover paper big enough to cover two boards with a 3 mm (⅛ in) gap between (A) and allowing for a 1.5 cm (⅝ in) turn-in around the outside edge (B).

Glue down the boards, leaving a 3 mm (⅛ in) joint allowance, or more for thick paper. If you are unsure about the right allowance to leave, fold a piece of the cover paper around two board thicknesses and crease. Add to this three thicknesses of lining paper and a little extra for the sewing (or more if you are using wire or rivets to attach the text panels).

Glue down the turn-ins at the board edges and the windows as described in step 12 for the 'Journal' on page 102.

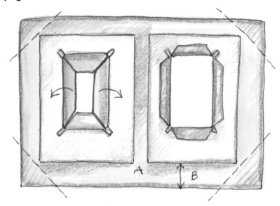

6

Make hinges from cloth or paper by folding the material in half and gluing it together. Then cut the hinges 3 mm (⅛ in) narrower than the panel at the head and tail (A). Glue one side of the hinge to one of the pairs.

7

Join the hinge to another pair of boards, allowing extra space between to accommodate a lining paper. Make sure there is no strain. The width of the hinges will vary, depending on the number of boards they have to fold around and what method you use to attach the text panels. In the 'Poem Book' on page 130, for example, three of the hinges wrap around two board thicknesses (A) and two of them have to accommodate three boards (B).

8

The fully extended model looks like this, with the hinges identified as described in the previous step.

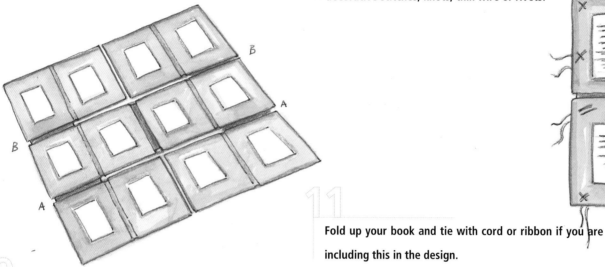

9

After the panels are joined together, line them with your chosen paper, following step 12 of the 'Journal' project, but this time taking the lining paper across any joints. Take extra care in rubbing down the paper between the joints or the book won't shut properly. Leave under a weight between waxed paper and pressing boards to dry.

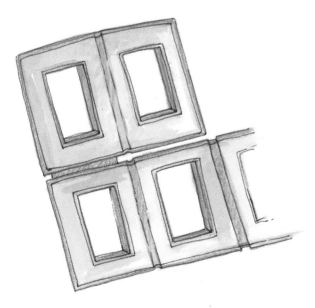

10

Attach your poem or text to the back of each panel using decorative stitches, knots, thin wire or rivets.

11

Fold up your book and tie with cord or ribbon if you are including this in the design.

12

If you prefer, the text (or photographs, drawings etc.) can be sandwiched between two sets of windows, but you will have to allow twice as much material for each hinge and at the board joints. If you decide to use this method, make two sets of windows following steps 4-7, and glue the panels with the text or image between. Press and leave to dry between waxed paper under weighted boards.

rebinding a book

there is no need to replace a favourite book
because it is falling apart.
You can repair it and turn it into a unique binding using
many of the techniques illustrated in this book.

The model shown here is a binding of *Alice in Wonderland* and *Alice through the Looking-Glass* sewn on wrapped raised cords. It has a window in the back board and onlays of Mexican bark paper. If you want to repair an old book that has lost its binding and don't want to include any artwork, follow steps 1 to 4 of this project and then follow steps 1 to 16 of the 'Case Binding' project on page 62. Finally, you can make a slipcase to protect your book as described on page 88 or perhaps a Japanese-style wrap-around case as shown on pages 38–40.

**The size of the book here is
20.1 x 13.7 x 3.5 cm (8¹⁄₁₆ x 5½ x 1³⁄₈ in).**

1

Take the book apart by first cutting the sewing threads in the middle of each signature carefully.

2

Place the book between pressing boards with a weight on top, leaving the spine protruding a little. For older books glued with animal glues, apply a thick layer of wheatflour paste to soften the old glue and leave to soak for a few minutes. Remove the old glue with a bone folder, being careful not to damage the damp paper. Remove all old sewing threads, tapes and lining materials as well. This method is not suitable for modern books with hot-melt adhesives on the spine.

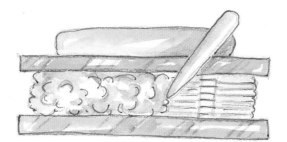

3

Cut tissue guards to repair sections, one for each signature (in the example on page 134 they are made from a thin Indian hand-made paper) slightly longer than the height and approximately 2 cm (¾ in) wider than the thickness of each signature. If you are repairing a book, you don't want the guards to show, so use a subtle Japanese tissue to match the book paper.

4

Lay the guards on a smooth work surface and apply paste to them one at a time. Attach to each signature, rub down well and leave to dry. You may find it easier to lay the guard on clean waxed paper once it is pasted and use the paper to wrap the guard around the signature to keep your hands clean. When the guards are dry, wrap the signatures in waxed paper and press overnight.

MATERIALS

Book to rebind

Japanese or Indian tissue or thin papers for the guards

Waxed paper for pressing

Thin greyboard

Waxed sewing thread

Cords or thongs for sewing supports

Endpapers

Cover paper

Artwork, photocopies, materials for onlays, acetate etc.

Cloth and paper for wrapper

PVA glue

Wheatflour paste

EQUIPMENT

Knife and/or scalpel

Cutting mat or board

Steel safety ruler

Dividers

Bone folder

Sewing needle

Hole punch (optional)

Glue and paste brushes

Pressing boards and a weight

5

Make holes in the signatures for sewing on cords, as described in steps 1 to 3 of 'Sewing over Cords or Thongs' page 50. The thread used in the model has been waxed and is wrapped around the cords a few times between coming out and going back into the sewing hole because the signatures are thick and a solid, red line was desired as part of the design.

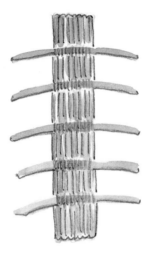

6

Then cut two endpapers slightly larger than the size of the book and tip them on as described in 'Attaching Endpapers' page 58. For extra strength, the blank leaf at the beginning of the book can be pasted to the first blank sheet of the book if there is one and pressed, using blotting paper to absorb some of the moisture. Change the blotting paper at regular intervals until the endpapers are dry. Trim to size.

7

Plan your design and cutouts since they need to be made before the boards are attached and covered. The circle used in the book on page 134 is a representation of either the rabbit hole or the looking-glass and has Alice, the Mad Hatter and the Cheshire Cat sandwiched between two sheets of acetate so you can see through to the other side. You can interpret your chosen book in many ways. For example, you could use the title as the design by enlarging and juggling the letter forms, or play around with embossing, illustrate a character or layer and sculpt the boards by using onlays. There is no right or wrong aspect for your design; just choose one you are interested in.

8

Cut four thin pieces of greyboard 3 mm (⅛ in) larger than the book at the head, tail and fore edge.

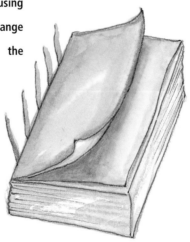

9

Once you have finalized your design, you can construct your cover boards. First, make the windows through the boards. Then glue on any raised elements of the design to the outer boards (see the 'Diary with a Clasp' project on page 122 for instructions on embossing) and make any necessary artwork, collage or onlays.

10

Cut two pieces of the coloured guard paper 2 cm (¾ in) longer than the height of the board and 1.5 cm (⅝ in) wide. Glue to the spine edge of the inner boards (A) and fold around the board edges at head and tail (B). Snip into the corners on both sides of the board and glue down the turn-ins (C).

11

Lay one of the inner boards in position with the covered edge in line with the back of the book. Fan out the cords and glue them to the boards. Repeat with the other board, then press with waxed paper and leave to dry under weighted boards.

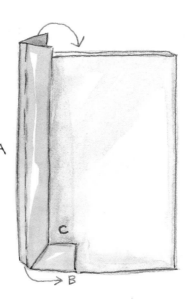

If you have cut windows into the boards, transfer their size and position to the endpaper by using a sharp pencil.

Cover the edges of any windows on the inner and outer boards with a strip of the coloured guard paper; snip and glue down to the board surfaces.

Cover the outer boards with your chosen material, pressing with a piece of sponge if you are embossing (see 'Diary with a Clasp' page 122). Trim the turn-ins to 2 cm (¾ in) on all four edges and cut the corners at the spine edge as indicated (A). Glue this turn-in down but leave the other three sides unglued at this point. The boards in the example on page 134 have their edges covered in paper to match the guards, with a panel of bark paper over the top. If you are using acetate between the boards, turn in the cover paper before gluing the boards together. If you just want a hole through the board to reveal an image on the endpaper, turn in the cover paper after the boards are laminated.

15

Lay your collage of images between the acetate sheets (cut slightly larger than the window) and position it on the inner board. Glue the outer boards and position them exactly over the top of the inner board. Press and leave the book to dry under a weight between waxed paper and pressing boards.

16

Trim the corners as usual and glue down the turn-ins over the laminated board edges.

17

While the boards are drying, prepare any other artwork you need for the cover. The book on page 134 has two onlays made from bark paper. Eyelets are applied with an eyelet punch and the 'eat me' and 'drink me' labels are threaded through and glued to the inside of the board.

18

Put a piece of waste board between the endpapers and support the cover board using pressing boards. Then cut out any windows previously marked. Also trim a sliver of paper away from the fore edge of the endpapers to allow for any stretch in the paper. Put down the endpapers as described in 'Case Binding' on page 62. Press and leave to dry under a weight between waxed paper and pressing boards.

suppliers

Acorn Art Shop
28 Colquhoun Street
Glasgow

Aitken Dott & Son
26 Castle Street
Edinburgh

Alexander of Newington
58 South Clerk Street
Edinburgh

The Arts Centre
71 Causeway Street
Paisley

The Arts Centre
583 Fishponds Road
Fishponds
Bristol

Art Repro
8 De-La-Beche Street
Swansea

The Art Shop
40 Castle Street
Guildford

The Art Shop
54 Castle Street
Trowbridge

The Art Shop
Great Coleman Street
Ipswitch

Atlantis Art Supplies
146 Brick Lane
London
E1 6RV

Binney & Smith
Ampthill Road
Bedford

The Blue Gallery
16 Joy Street
Barnstaple

H. Blyth & Co.
53 Back George Street
Manchester

Brentwood Arts
106 London Road
Stockton Heath
Warrington

Briggs Art & Book Shop
15 Crouch Street
Colchester

The Chantry Studios
Pauls Row
High Wycombe

Cowling & Wilcox
26 Broadwick Street
London, WI

Dahle (UK) Ltd
37 Camford Way
Luton
Beds, LU3 3AN

Daler Board Co. Ltd.
Wareham, Dorset

J. Davey & Sons Ltd.
70 Bridge Street
Manchester

The Dollar Gallery
22 West Burnside
Glasgow

J. B. Duckett & Co Ltd
74 Bradfield Road
Sheffield

Falcon Art Supplies Ltd.
26 George Street
Pestwich

Ivor Fields
21 Stert Street
Abingdon
Oxfordshire

W Frank Gadsby Ltd.
9 Bradford Street
Walsall

Fred Aldus Ltd
37 Lever Street
Manchester

Greyfriars Art Shop
1 Greyfriars Place
Edinburgh

Gordons Gallery
152 Victoria Road
Scarborough

Handyman
43 Tamworth Street
Lichfield

E. Hopper & Co. Ltd.
48 Market Place
Malton
Yorks

Langford & Hill
10 Warwick Street
London W1

Liverpool Fine Arts
85a Bold Street
Liverpool

Llanelli Art Centre
31 Market Street
Llanelli

Mair & Son
46 The Strand
Exmouth

John Mathieson & Co
48 Frederick Street
Edinburgh

A. Perkin & Son
2a Bletchington Road
Hove

Reeves & Sons Ltd
Lincoln Road
Enfield
Middx

Reeves Arts Materials
178 Kensington High Street
London W8

C. Roberson & Co Ltd
71 Parkway
London NW1

George Rowney & Co Ltd
P.O. Box 10
Bracknell
Berks

George Rowney & Co Ltd
121 Percy Street
London W1

Russell & Chapple
23 Monmouth Street
London WC2H 9DE

Studio 10
10 Edleston Road
Crewe

Torbay Art and Craft Centre
109 Union Street
Torquay

Trinity Galleries
Trinity Street
Colchester

Windsor & Newton
P.O. Box 91
Wealdstone
Harrow, Middx

BOOKBINDING MATERIALS AND EQUIPMENT

J. Hewit & Sons Ltd
Unit 28, Par Royal Metro Centre
Britannia Way
London NW10 7PR
0181 965 5377

Ratchford Bookcraft Supplies Ltd
Kennedy Way
Green Lane
Stockport
Cheshire SK4 2JX
0161 480 8484

Russell Bookcrafts
Great North Road
Wyboston
Bedfordshire MK44 3AB
01480 405464

Bookbinding Equipment
Sally Martin
9 Marsh Road
Oulton Road, Lowestoft
Suffolk NR33 9JY

Shepherds Bookbinders Ltd
76b Rochester Row
London SW1P 1JU
9171 630 1184

Harmatan Leather Ltd
Westfield Avenue
Higham Ferrers
Northampton NN9 8AX
01933 12471/412151

PAPER SUPPLIES

Ann Muir Marbling
1 St Algar's Yard
West Woodlands
Frome
Somerset BA11 5ER
01985 844786

Cockerell Marbled Papers
94 Wimpole Road
Barton
Cambridge CB3 7AD
01223 262430

Falkiner Fine Papers
76 Southampton Row
London WC1 4AR

John Purcell Paper
15 Rumsey Road
London SW9 0TR
0171 737 5199

Paperchase
216 Tottenham Court Road
London W1
0171 637 1121

Paperpoint
130 Longacre
London WC2 9AL
0171 379 6850

GENERAL

The Bead Shop
43 Neal Street
Covent Garden
London WC2H 9JP
0171 240 0831

USEFUL ADDRESSES

Designer Bookbinders
6 Queen Square
London WC1 3AR

The Society of Bookbinders
Lower Hammonds Farm
Ripley Lane
West Horsley
Surrey KT24 6JP

The British Library
96 Euston Road
London NW1 2DB

Crafts Council
44a Pentonville Road
Islington
London N1 9BY
0171 278 7700

selected bibliography

Chambers, Anne.
A Practical Guide to Marbling Paper.
Thames & Hudson, London. 1986

Chambers, Anne.
Suminagashi. The Japanese Art of Marbling.
Thames and Hudson, London. 1991

Cockerell, D.
Bookbinding and the Care of Books.
Pitman, London and New York. 1963

Ikegami, Kojiro.
Japanese Bookbinding.
Weatherhill, New York. 1986

Ipert, Stephane & Rousseau, Florent.
Simple Decorative Paper Techniques. Search Press, London. 1992

Johnson, Arthur W.
Thames and Hudson Manual of Bookbinding.
Thames and Hudson, London. 1978

La Plantz, Shereen.
Cover to Cover.
Lark Books, 1995

Larbalestier, Simon.
The Art and Craft of Montage.
Mitchell Beazley, London. 1993

Middleton, Bernard.
A History of English Craft Bookbinding Technique.
Hafner Press, London. 1963

Ploughman, John
The Craft of Handmade Paper.
Apple Press, London. 1997

Robinson, Ivor
Introducing Bookbinding.
Oxford Polytechnic Press, London and New York. 1984

Saddington, Marianne.
Making Your Own Paper.
New Holland Ltd, London. 1990

Shannon, Faith.
The Art and Craft of Paper.
Mitchell Beazley, London. 1987

Smith, Keith A.
Non-Adhesive Binding Volume 1. Books Without Paste or Glue.
Keith Smith Books, New York. 1993

Smith, Keith A.
Non-Adhesive Binding Volume 2. 1,2 & 3 Section Sewings.
Keith Smith Books, New York. 1995

Smith, Keith A.
Non-Adhesive Binding Volume 3. Exposed Spine Sewings.
Keith Smith Books, New York. 1996

Smith, Keith A.
Structure of the Visual Book.
Keith Smith Books, New York. 1994

Smith, Keith A.
Text in the Book Format.
Keith Smith Books, New York. 1995

Smith, Philip.
The Book: Art and Object.
Philip Smith, Merstham. 1992

Smith, Philip.
New Directions in Bookbinding.
Studio Vista, London and New York. 1974

The New Bookbinder. The Journal of Designer Bookbinders Volumes 1-17.
Published annually by Designer Bookbinders, London.

Turner, Silvie.
Which Paper?
Estamp, London. 1991

Turner, Silvie and Birgit Skiold.
Handmade Paper Today.
Lund Humphries, London. 1985

Watson, David.
Creative Handmade Paper.
Search Press, London. 1991

Williams, Nancy.
Paperwork.
Phaidon Press, London. 1993

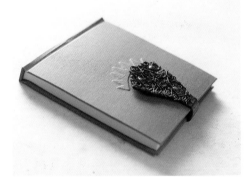

credits

Gallery 1 (pages 34-35)
Left to Right: Mary Deakin 'Tyger, Tyger' by William Blake; Sue Doggett 'Eel Corridor'
'The Cheese Musem'; Flutter Book; Fold-Out Book

Gallery 2 (pages 44-45)
Left to Right: Clare Bryan 'Forbidden Fruit'; (Top to Bottom) Emma Ruffle, Sue Doggett, Emma Ruffle, Emma Ruffle, Sue Doggett; Sue Doggett 'Serpents and Skulls';
Emma Ruffle; Sue Doggett

Gallery 3 (pages 70-71)
Left to Right: Vivien Frank 'Bestiary'; Sue Doggett; (standing) Sue Doggett, (flat) Penny Stanford; (Top to bottom) Vivien Frank, Vivien Frank, Sue Doggett; Sue Doggett

Gallery 4 (pages 80-81)
Left to Right: (left) Sue Whittington (Right) Margaret Benson; Clare Bryan 'Alice in Wonderland'; Sue Doggett; Sue Doggett 'Inamorato'; (left) Helen Hutchins, (right) Penny Stanford

Gallery 5 (pages 92-93)
Left to Right: Clare Bryan 'Open Closed'; Clare Bryan 'Open Closed'; Helen Hutchins; Emma Ruffle; Sue Doggett 'Mr Palomar's Library'

acknowledgments

I would like to thank the following people for their support over the years and during the writing of this book.

To all my teachers and colleagues for introducing me to the book as an exciting medium with which to work, also for sharing their hard-earned knowledge and creative energy with me and hundreds of other students.
Thanks go especially to Ivor Robinson, who has taught me so much, helped me out of sticky situations and gave me my first teaching job. To members of Designer Bookbinders who have offered advice and support, particularly David Sellars, Jenni Grey, and Faith Shannon (who have taught me how to make the majority of bindings in this book), Jen Lindsay, Romilly Saumarez-Smith and Philip Smith, all of whom have been hugely influential creatively as colleagues and as friends.

Special thanks to Maggie Chandler who was so supportive as a colleague and so generous in sharing her teaching methods with me. Thanks also to her, for showing me how to make the 'Wrap-around Book' (page 38) and the 'Limp Paper Binding' (page 66).

Many thanks to Hedi Kyle whose 'Flag Book' (page 76) and 'Everlasting Fold Book' (page 28) are included with her kind permission. It is thanks to people like Hedi Kyle for popularizing book structures like the 'Star Book' and the 'Theatre Book' which are now standards in the book artist's repertoire.

Thanks to all the past and present students who kindly lent work to be photographed for this book, and special thanks to Pauline Brown for suggesting the thread work on the 'Fold-Out Book' (page 31) and which I have incorporated in the 'Poem Book'.

Kind thanks to Rob Shepherd of Shepherd Bookbinders Ltd, for lending materials and equipment for the photographs in the introductory chapters.

Many thanks to Emma Ruffle of John Purcell Paper for advice and suggestions on interesting and unusual papers.

Thanks to my family for supporting and encouraging me always, and to Clare for her artistic support and advice.

Finally, a grateful and very special thanks to Jonathan for his constant support, enthusiasm and patience, and for keeping my confidence going.

index